Interpreting Bach's *Well-Tempered Clavier*

Interpreting Bach's
Well-Tempered Clavier
A Performer's Discourse of Method

Ralph Kirkpatrick

Yale University Press
New Haven and London

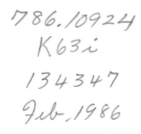
Ralph Kirkpatrick's original Deutsche Grammophon harpsichord recordings of the *Well-Tempered Clavier* have been reissued. The complete five-disk set is available exclusively through Quarry Communications and Distributing, P. O. Box 3168, Stony Creek, Connecticut 06405.

Designed by Nancy Ovedovitz and set in Times Roman type by Graphic Composition, Inc. Printed in the United States of America by Murray Printing Company, Westford, Massachusetts.

Library of Congress Cataloging in Publication Data
Kirkpatrick, Ralph.
  Interpreting Bach's Well-tempered clavier.
  Includes index.
  1. Bach, Johann Sebastian, 1685–1750. Wohltemperierte Klavier. I. Title. II. Title: Well-tempered clavier.
MT145.B14K57   1984   786.1′092′4   84–5811
ISBN: 0–300–03058–4

10   9   8   7   6   5   4   3   2   1

Ainsi mon dessein n'est pas d'enseigner ici la méthode que chacun doit suivre pour bien conduire sa raison, mais seulement de faire voir en quelle sorte j'ai tâché de conduire la mienne.

René Descartes
Discours de la méthode, I

Contents

Chapter IV.
The Rhythmic Approach   65

Chapter V.
The Harmonic Approach   89

Musical Examples

Preface

When in 1964 I was asked to inaugurate the Ernest Bloch Visiting Professorship at the University of California at Berkeley, I decided to organize my visit around *The Well-Tempered Clavier* with the recording and numerous performances of which I was then engaged. In addition to complete performances of the *WTC* on both harpsichord and clavichord, and various classes, I gave the six lectures, repeated the following year at Yale, which form the basis of this little book. Because most of the lectures were accompanied from the keyboard by an almost constant flow of musical illustration, it was foreseeable that many revisions would be required to convert them into a publishable book. In the subsequent years these revisions were delayed by extensive concert commitments, by the recording sessions for both versions of Book II of the *WTC*, by the drudgery attendant upon my facsimile edition of the complete sonatas of Scarlatti and, after its publication in 1972, by various convalescences.

Concerning the last major revision undertaken a few months before my total loss of sight in 1976, I came to agree with the publishers that this version of the lectures was by no means ready for publication. It was only when I was approached by Edward Tripp of Yale University Press that the prospect of a high and helpful degree of editorial proximity presented itself. The manuscript was given to a reader (whose identity is still unknown to me) with whose highly perceptive comments and criticism I found myself in almost total agreement. Once again I subjected the manuscript to a long and understandably difficult set of revisions.

In no way does this book resemble any of the others that have been written about *The Well-Tempered Clavier*. It differs in virtually every respect from anything that might appear to have a comparable title. Factual history, esthetic speculation, and systematic analysis are admitted here only as they directly concern a player who is actively dealing with this music. It makes no pretense to a complete verbal exposition of the *WTC* in terms of program notes or prescriptions for the performance of each piece. It points out instead many of the ways which its reader may choose for augmenting and deepening his perceptions not only of the *WTC* but of all music.

In this respect the central chapters concerning melody, rhythm, and harmony constitute the book's most important parts. To them the two opening chapters and even the last chapter might be regarded as mere appendages. I have not attempted to anticipate the historical and critical material that will become available when the *WTC* and its accompanying text revision is published in the *Neue Bach Ausgabe*. Nor have I been occupied with structural analysis of the kind that has already been expounded in many books on the subject. Much of the vast literature already published about the *WTC* deserves either oblivion or that kind of specific attack in which I am here unwilling to engage. Hence the absence of a conventional bibliography selected from the hundreds of entries accumulated during my initial preparations. Where necessary I have given source references in footnotes which, like the text, are covered by the general index. Musical examples from the *WTC* are drawn from the edition by Franz Kroll published in Vol. XIV of the Bachgesellschaft edition and reprinted in reduced format by Lea Pocket Scores. It is to be hoped that by the time of publication my recordings of both books of the *WTC* on both harpsichord and clavichord, respectively for Deutsche Grammophon and for Archiv, will have been reissued.

Over the years I have learned from composers, conductors, instrumentalists, and singers much that inevitably reflects itself here, and particularly from such musicians as Diran Alexanian, Artur Schnabel, and George Szell so much that were they still alive they would receive—like Hindemith and Stravinsky[1]—specially dedicated copies of this book. Among the living there are performers, singers, and conductors who exemplify the best of what I have tried to set forth in the following pages. It suffices to hear but a few measures of their performances to be assured that they have really heard and are still

---

1. Kirkpatrick, Ralph: "Recollections of Two Composers: Hindemith and Stravinsky," *The Yale Review*, Vol. 71 [July 1982], pp. 627–640.

listening to what is in the music they play. Indeed, they have so little need for this book that it can only be offered to them in tribute. It is a further cause for joy to reflect that many of these superb musicians are now scarcely above thirty years of age. However, there are conductors, singers, and instrumentalists whose performances need but a few measures to demonstrate that a further training of ear and perceptions such as is discussed in these pages would be sorely needed. Many of them are in high places and there is little likelihood that this book would have done or could ever do them any good even if their success, whatever its reasons, were not so great as to preclude both time and inclination to make its acquaintance.

Aside from those performers who have no need of the following pages, and from those who lack the time and inclination to consult them, there is a further category of musicians whose capacity for self-teaching and for further development is inexhaustible. It is on such people as they, and I presume to include myself among them, that my hopes depend. For them, despite the erosion of my once excessively optimistic view of education, this pedagogical testament, this discourse of method is designed.

Acknowledgements are due to Alan Curtis, who first proposed this series of lectures, to Joseph Kerman, who was my academic host at the time of the original lectures, and to the many others who gave help and encouragement during my stay in Berkeley in 1964. Frederick Hammond gave one more proof of his inexhaustible generosity in reading onto tape the 1982 version of this book. The staff of the Library of the Yale School of Music, most particularly Harold Samuel and Victor Cardell, stood ready as usual to respond to every need. On behalf of the Yale University Press, valuable help was received from Dennis Libby, Christopher Haley, and most of all from Thomas Christensen, who took charge of the final preparation of the musical examples. Christian Foy taught his computer to speak in order that I might be supplied with a talking typewriter. My secretary, Shirley Mack, who typed the manuscript, showed her unflagging loyalty and patience in reading over and over to me those passages requiring revisions, and in helping me to check the revisions themselves.

February 1984
Guilford, Connecticut

Introduction

My purpose here is not so much to expound *The Well-Tempered Clavier* as to examine almost every method of interpretative approach to music that has been useful to me as a player or as a teacher. The result of this examination has become a kind of *Discours de la méthode* of a performing musician. Like a ground swell under the following chapters runs the notion that every question, every problem, every sentiment must be examined, compared, and experienced by the individual interpreter rather than taken at face value or imposed by hearsay or by tradition.

When in 1953 I devised the curious little catechism that prefaces my edition of sixty Scarlatti sonatas,[1] I tried to set down every question I could recall ever having asked in the course of working out an interpretation, routining a performance, or coaching a pupil. Had I been editing Bach at the time instead of Scarlatti, this catechism could have served just as well. Its principles find an even richer and more closely applicable exposition in relation to Bach's *Well-Tempered Clavier*. Yet I might equally well have written in the same terms while drawing my examples from the sonatas and other music of Haydn, Mozart, and Beethoven, or even by restricting them to the Impromptus of Schubert, the Preludes and Etudes of Chopin, or to almost any Western music down to the present day.

Although many of the techniques of analysis expounded here demand an initial approach that is deliberately conscious, their only value lies in their ability to become absorbed in that unconscious

---

1. Scarlatti, Domenico: *Sixty Sonatas . . . Edited . . . with a preface by Ralph Kirkpatrick*. New York, G. Schirmer [1953].

network of feelings, associations, and prior experience that within itself is constantly readjusting everything to everything else.

In the following pages I may be unable to avoid offering a kind of idealized *Portrait of the Artist in His Studio*. Not only have I sketched the manner in which I work, but I have also outlined many ideals which I may or may not have achieved. For the moment, however, it is perhaps better to assume that the portrait, though idealized, is a composite portrait embodying what one would most desire in an interpreter.

From time to time I may appear to pontificate, but I can only say that such is not my intention, and that my hope is to enlighten rather than to prove a point. If I seem to allude too frequently to my own interpretations or if I seem unduly partial to them, it is because they furnish my most convenient examples, even though this exposition of working methods is designed also to be valuable for the forming of interpretations quite different from my own. We will attempt to approach the source of our examples, the *WTC*, rather than to capture it. I cannot insist too much that this is a set of suggested methods rather than a system. The appearance of a system is only the result of necessary devices of organization. Much of what I shall be discussing will sound disconcertingly theoretical, but its intellectuality is in no way intended as a substitute for inspiration. It aims to help make use of inspiration, and to help inspiration guide and perpetuate itself.

Our principal approaches—melodic, rhythmic, and harmonic—are made in the belief that music only comes to life when arousing directly or imaginatively the activities and functions of the human body. Sound that does not penetrate beyond the ear into the entire physical and nervous organism is not music. Sound is perceived by the ear, music by the entire being.

As I wrote in my Scarlatti preface:

> For me the working out of a musical interpretation or the solving of a technical problem is inseparable from the necessary life-long process of training the ear. No ear is so dull that it cannot be trained; no ear is so sensitive that it cannot be taught or teach itself to hear more; no emotional capacities or sensory perceptions are so complete that they cannot be further developed. In every piece of worthwhile music there is always something that can still be discovered, always something that will

have escaped its most experienced and most sensitive performer. Any interpreter who is not a parrot-performer knows
the experience of sudden revelation or of gradual new light on
a piece he may have already played for many years. Yet many
of these revelations and new undertakings need not await the
accident of circumstances or the passage of time. Often they
can be brought about by a few provocative comparisons or by a
few simple self-imposed questions.

In the course of this work many possible methods of approach
will be excluded from discussion because they do not appear to contribute to the direct experiencing and interpreting of the music. Much
that is valuable to the composer and to the theorist is not necessarily
directly useful to the performer. By and large, the performer is dealing with a musical construction that has already been made by the
composer. His responsibility is to understand the existing construction and to render it intelligible. Nevertheless, the composer and the
performer share a disciplined approach to a piece of music, as I
indicated in my Scarlatti preface:

> As every composer and writer knows, there is no better way of
> finding out what one really feels than having to set it down on
> paper, or having to communicate it through an artificial and
> restricted medium. A composer cannot write down an orchestral
> score without having eliminated every element of the haphazard
> and non-organic; he has to do much more than merely float on
> the seas of his own emotions. He must adopt definite concrete
> means of conveying those emotions through a medium over which
> he no longer has any direct control, nor any control at all other
> than the manner in which he has set his notes down on paper.
> The performer's problem is less formidable, but similar. He
> must be able to marshal the spontaneity of his sensations into a
> consistent, ordered performance which he can produce at any
> time and under any circumstances. To this end, he must sense
> what elements of a piece are fixed and unchangeable in their
> relationship to each other, what is basic syntax and structure,
> and what is mere rhetorical inflection, what can be improvised
> and altered from performance to performance. Only by this se-
> curity in relation to basic musical elements can he achieve true
> freedom and spontaneity in performance. The ability to make

departures depends on a thorough knowledge of what one is departing from.

The three approaches, melodic, rhythmic, and harmonic, employ disciplines that are designed to make sure that not a single note of any piece will have remained overlooked, unheard, or unrelated to its context. They are not intended to prescribe a specific interpretation, but they provide the materials for a wide variety of possible interpretations. The multiple levels on which they function and of their interactions create a musical material of such richness and flexibility that the interpreter is left a freedom of choice qualified only by the fundamental proportions and limitations of the work itself. This presupposes the cultivation to a high degree of what one can only call musical literacy.

I have always regarded musical literacy as making it possible to break things down into their elements, to put them together again, and to spell them out in the context of those rules of grammar that in any language enable communication. Literacy is obviously an enormous aid to freedom of thought. It enables one to remember what one has already thought, to perpetuate it, and to compare it, but as the last five hundred years of history have shown us, literacy is by no means a guarantee of freedom. It can also lead to the perpetuation and acceptance of platitudes and unexamined ideas. It lends itself just as much to human laziness as to human industry.

Simply because a name has been tacked onto something, it can easily be thought to have been understood; once an idea has been formulated, it is all too easy to make up the mind and close it. To all of these activities, literacy is unfortunately an aid. But when used in conjunction with imagination, it is indeed a liberating force. It is imagination that makes it possible to recombine all sorts of elements and tendencies in new and unforeseen forms. Nowhere in this *discours de la méthode* can be found an absolute guarantee of a good interpretation, much less of a good performance. It is only a contribution to the techniques of producing these results, an exposé of a set of methods. But these methods can be misused just as much as they can be used. The useful employment of these methods must necessarily depend on that power which all of us have within us to experience and to recompose the materials of experience. There is hardly a human being who is entirely devoid of imagination, if he will but allow himself to function imaginatively.

CHAPTER I.

The Historical Approach
and Its Limitations

ORIGINS OF *THE WELL-TEMPERED CLAVIER*, BOOK I · MEANING OF
THE TERM *CLAVIER* · ORIGINS OF BOOK II · EDITIONS · BACH'S TEXT ·
EARLY AND LATER FASHIONS IN PLAYING BACH · A NEW SEARCH FOR
BACH · LITERATURE ABOUT *THE WELL-TEMPERED CLAVIER*

Origins of *The Well-Tempered Clavier*, Book I

We know very little of the origin of Book I of the *WTC*. Ernst Ludwig Gerber, however, recalls the experiences of his father, Heinrich Nikolaus, with the *WTC* while studying with Bach. His father had evidently been told that Bach had composed the *WTC* in a relatively short time, while in a place where he had no instrument at his disposal and where he had nothing else to do.[1] Gerber also recalls that his father said that on several occasions, instead of giving him a lesson, Bach had resorted to playing the preludes and fugues of the *WTC*. Gerber says that his father heard them from Bach at least three times.[2] He does not say whether he heard all of both books. These stories perhaps should not be taken as statements of actual fact. There is evidence that the composition of the *WTC* took place over a longer span of time than supposed. Gerber's recollection of three complete performances is one that might well have been exaggerated in retrospect.

---

1. Gerber, E. L.: *Historisch-Biographisches Lexicon der Tonkünstler . . . Erster Theil A-M*, Leipzig, Johann Gottlob Immanuel Breitkopf, 1790, p. 90.
2. Gerber, p. 491.

The evidence of earlier versions of pieces in Book I appears principally in the *Clavier-Büchlein vor Wilhelm Friedemann Bach*,[3] the little collection of pieces that Bach put together for his eldest son and dated 1720, two years before the date of the earliest known compilation of Book I. Eleven of the preludes appear there, in some cases incompletely copied out and in other cases in shorter versions. A number of them, such as the D minor and E minor preludes, lack the extensions that are familiar to us in their later forms, and numerous small modifications would further indicate that the process of composition was not necessarily confined to one brief period.

In 1722 Bach assembled the first of the two collections of twenty-four preludes and fugues under the following title:

Das Wohl temperierte Clavier oder Praeludia und Fugen durch alle Tone und Semitonia Sowohl tertiam majorem oder Ut Re Mi anlangend, als auch tertiam minorem oder Re Mi Fa betreffend. Zum Nutzen und Gebrauch der Lehrbegierigen Musicalischen Jugend als auch derer in diesem studio schon habil seyenden besondern Zeit Vertreib aufgesetzet und verfertiget von Johann Sebastian Bach p.t. Hochfurstl. Anhalt. Cothenischen Capell-Meistern und Directore derer Cammer-Musiquen. Anno 1722.[4]

(The Well-Tempered Clavier, or preludes and fugues in all tones and semitones, in major as well as minor, for the benefit and use of musical youth desirous of knowledge as well as those who are already advanced in this study. For their especial diversion, composed and prepared by Johann Sebastian Bach, currently ducal chapelmaster in Anhalt-Cöthen and director of chamber music, in the year 1722.)

Bach's title has given rise to much discussion. The term *well-tempered* refers to a system of tuning which adjusts the natural intervals of the harmonic series of overtones to the restrictions of a

3. Library of the Yale School of Music. Johann Sebastian Bach, *Clavier-Büchlein vor Wilhelm Friedemann Bach*, edited in facsimile with a preface by Ralph Kirkpatrick. New Haven, Yale University Press, 1959.
4. Berlin, Deutsche Staatsbibliothek, Mus. Ms. autogr. Bach P415. Published in facsimile by Deutscher Verlag für Musik, Leipzig [1962]. At the end of this manuscript is the date 1732, presumably the date of its copying.

twelve-note chromatic scale in such fashion that all of the twelve major and minor keys are playable.[5] To make a circle of fifths close where it began, every fifth has to be reduced or tempered. Some tuners count beats as a way of checking the equality of their tempered fifths. Others, like myself, tune by ear and check with other intervals. A work of Johann Caspar Ferdinand Fischer, the *Ariadne* of 1702 (first known edition 1715),[6] actually uses twenty different tonalities. It avoids only those most remote from C major. And in Mattheson's thoroughbass treatise, the *Exemplarische Organisten-Probe* of 1719 (republished in 1731 in an expanded version as the *Grosse General-Bass-Schule*) we find practice examples for figured-bass players in all of the twenty-four major and minor keys.

Systems of tuning more closely attached to the pure fifths and thirds of the natural overtone series either require more intervals than the twelve-note octave of the ordinary keyboard affords, unless given special subdivisions, or they favor only certain tonalities. This explains the infrequency in older music of tonalities involving more than three or four sharps and flats. So-called pure intonation based on the natural intervals is still instinctive to every good musician and is still commonly practiced by string players and singers. Thus, for example, in pure intonation, a rising G-sharp functioning as a leading tone would differ from a descending A-flat. The conventional keyboard, however, gives the same sound for both notes, creating a compromise to which the sensitive musical ear has only reluctantly become accustomed.

Actually, as I can testify from my own experience as a tuner of keyboard instruments, the ear will accept a number of gradients between an exact equal temperament and a tuning based on a mixture of pure and impure intervals. It must be remembered that all keyboard intonation in any system is subject to instinctive correction in terms of the musical context. The establishment of equal temperament was far more important as a principle permitting a wider range of tonalities than as a change in actual practice. Its principle, how-

5. For a comprehensive account and bibliography, see Lindley, Mark: "Temperaments," in *The New Grove Dictionary of Music and Musicians* [London, 1980], Vol. 18, pp. 660–674.
6. Fischer, Johann Caspar Ferdinand: *Sämtliche Werke für Klavier und Orgel . . .* Herausgegeben von Ernst v. Werra. Leipzig [Preface dated 1901].

ever, received categorical reinforcement, and its practice further encouragement from such works as the *WTC*.

A well-documented and carefully reasoned article by John Barnes,
"Bach's Keyboard Temperament, Internal Evidence from *The Well-
Tempered Clavier*,"[7] cannot be overlooked, despite its arrival at conclusions that might be considered to limit excessively a conception
of Bach's creative process and of the functioning of his inner musical
ear. My reaction on belated discovery of this article has been like
that of Molière's hero, M. Jourdain, who finds solace in the confir-
mation that all along he has been talking in prose. In fifty years of
tuning harpsichords and clavichords with no other aid than a tuning
fork and my own ear and without benefit of mathematical calcula-
tions and systems, I have arrived at adjustments of the twelve-note
octave that are remarkably similar. They can be heard in my self-
tuned recordings of the clavichord version of both books of the *WTC*
and of the harpsichord version of Book II.

Meaning of the Term *Clavier*

That part of Bach's title which has raised the most controversy is the
word *clavier*, especially because of the transformations undergone
in its various translations. There is no evidence whatever to permit
interpreting Bach's use of the word as indicating anything other than
the general term *keyboard*, in other words any keyboard instrument.
This use of the term to embrace all three of the principal keyboard
instruments of the time is graphically illustrated in the prefatory en-
gravings of Kuhnau's *Clavier-Übung* of 1689, the *Frische Clavier
Früchte* of 1696, and the *Biblische Historien* of 1700, where repre-
sentations appear, respectively, of a harpsichord, clavichord, and a
chamber organ.[8] Although some works of Bach are designated for
harpsichord or organ, most of his keyboard music bears no desig-

7. Barnes, John: "Bach's Keyboard Temperament, Internal Evidence from *The Well-
Tempered Clavier*," *Early Music*, Vol. 7 [April 1979], pp. 236–249. See also
Blood, William: "'Well-Tempering' the Clavier: Five Methods," *Early Music*,
Vol. 7 [October 1979], pp. 491–495.
8. Title pages reproduced in facsimile in reprint: Kuhnau, Johann: *Johann Kuhnaus
Klavierwerke*. Edited by Karl Päsler in *Denkmäler deutscher Tonkunst*, Vol. 4.
Leipzig, Breitkopf & Härtel, 1901.

nation more specific than that for clavier. By the time of the publication of Carl Philipp Emanuel Bach's *Versuch* in 1753 the term *clavier* had come to be reserved for the clavichord, and the harpsichord was called *Clavicimbel* or *Flügel* or *Kielflügel*. The change in meaning of the term *clavier* probably accounts for the different translations of the title of the *WTC*. In France it has always been known as *Le clavecin bien temperé*, and in Italy as *Il clavicembalo ben temperato*; only in the English-speaking world is it known as *The Well-Tempered Clavichord*. In the earliest English publication of the *WTC*, where it is simply called *Forty-Eight Preludes and Fugues*, there is no mention of the clavichord.[9] But certainly ever since the middle of the last century the reference to the clavichord has predominated in the English-speaking world.[10]

Bach's own designations of specific keyboard instruments are exceedingly rare. The organ is the instrument most frequently indicated. Among the works commonly attributed to the harpsichord, Bach has definitely specified the Italian Concerto, the French Ouverture, and the Goldberg Variations for the two-manual harpsichord. He makes no specific designation for the Partitas, for the English and French Suites, for the Inventions, or for the *WTC*.

Although there is a certain amount of eighteenth-century German writing about harpsichords and their construction, a remarkably small number of instruments have survived and we know far less about German harpsichords than we know about those of any other school. While a better knowledge would throw light on the interpretation of many keyboard works of Bach, I doubt that it would reveal much that would be directly pertinent to the *WTC*. The notions that are pertinent to the *WTC* are not necessarily dependent on the kind of instrument that is used. Some of the pieces permit a wide range of choice among the instrumental colors as represented by the choice of registers on the harpsichord. Some pieces may be regarded as inherently *forte* and others as inherently *piano*, and others appear to have the possibility of being either *forte* or *piano*. They can be con-

9. *S. Wesley and C. F. Horn's New and Correct Edition of the Preludes and Fugues, of John Sebastian Bach* . . . London, Birchall [*c*. 1813?].

10. Actually, I am acquainted only with the undated publication by Novello, London and with the publications [G. Schirmer, New York] of the edition of Czerny (1893) and that of Book I by Busoni (1894).

sidered to sound equally as well when played on solo instruments as when played with all the doublings of an orchestral tutti. Among the solistic pieces are some that may be considered to sound better when played on two manuals. There is little, in my view, in the *WTC* which permits a change of registration within the course of a single piece. (An occasional shift of manuals, as in the echo effects of the Prelude in G-sharp minor of Book II, can only be regarded as exceptional.)

The concept of Bach's harpsichord has been badly obscured by the century-old legend of the "Bach instrument" in Berlin. In 1860 this instrument was first brought to public attention in Wilhelm Rust's preface to volume IX of the Bachgesellschaft edition. Although it never did belong to the Bach family, it came to be regarded as a typical Bach instrument. It now has eight- and four-foot on the upper manual and eight- and sixteen-foot on the lower, with a shove coupler and a buff stop for the upper eight-foot. Until recent years at least ninety percent of modern harpsichord building in Germany was influenced by this "Bach instrument." Friedrich Ernst has proved not only that the four-foot was originally on the lower manual but that the sixteen-foot was actually a later addition to the instrument.[11] This removes the foundation from much theorizing about the treatment of Bach's harpsichord works, and any claim of authenticity from much still-current practice. It also invalidates the recommendations for registration in the preface to my 1938 edition of the Goldberg Variations.[12] Because I no longer feel that any prelude or fugue of the *WTC* requires internal changes of registration (except for the echo effects of the Prelude in G-sharp minor II), I shall not discuss choices of tone color as affected by registration. While registration, like any satisfactory instrumentation, is important in enhancing the character of a piece, much more is to be deduced from an examination of Bach's own orchestration than from any necessarily subjective principles of registration that I might attempt to enunciate here.

11. Ernst, Friedrich: *Der Flügel Joh. Seb. Bachs* . . . C. F. Peters, Frankfurt, London, New York, 1955.
12. Bach, J. S.: *Keyboard Practice consisting of an Aria with thirty variations for the harpsichord with 2 manuals* . . . edited for the harpsichord or piano by Ralph Kirkpatrick. New York, G. Schirmer [1938].

For many years, I had the unrealized and now unrealizable ambition to undertake a performance of the *WTC* on an organ of suitable characteristics. I also would have found it entertaining to undertake a performance on the piano. For that matter, I would rather hear a good performance on the piano than a bad one on either the harpsichord or the clavichord. (I must admit, however, that while I have heard at various times some of the preludes and fugues admirably played on the piano, I have never heard either in concert or on records a complete performance that I could commend.)

I believe it impossible to claim irrefutably that any part of the *WTC* belongs exclusively to any one keyboard instrument, whether harpsichord, clavichord, or organ. Historical and stylistic evidence lends itself to arguments in several directions, none of them conclusive. The preludes and fugues are works that take on different aspects according to the medium in which they are executed. Furthermore, their implications reach far beyond the confines of any mere keyboard instrument. Just as drawings are often sketches of paintings, so are many of the fugues suggestions of choral works. As a drawing in a painter's sketchbook may prefigure an enormous fresco, so a keyboard fugue of the *WTC* may suggest a massive *Kyrie*. The seemingly ridiculous undertaking of giving to a non-sustaining keyboard instrument the four or five voices of a sustained vocal fugue explains itself if we understand that suggestion, as in poetry and drawing, can sometimes be more powerful and stimulating to the imagination than downright statement.

In accordance with the varying proportions of suggestion, especially in Book I of the *WTC*, there is a considerable discrepancy of size among individual pieces, for example, the tiny Prelude that precedes the enormous A minor Fugue, or the widely differing scale, as in an artist's sketchbook, of the small E major Prelude and Fugue, and the great D-sharp minor Fugue that precedes.

There exists in the *WTC*, especially in the first book, a certain discrepancy between the sketchbooklike haphazardness and diversity of its contents and the rigorous formalism of its organization. The preludes and fugues of the *WTC* are organized in terms of an idea; they respond to a theoretical and pedagogical challenge that in a lesser composer might have smothered the infinite eloquence of their utterances as works of art. The arrangement of the preludes and fugues is a bringing into logical order, not a dramatic sequence. The impact of a total performance of the *WTC*, when other than soporific, is that of a literally overwhelming variety and richness, not that of an organized progression from one piece to another. In certain highly organized works of Bach such as the Goldberg Variations or the organ works of the *Clavier-Übung*, I believe it is just barely possible to make directly and dramatically perceptible to the ear the almost superhuman organization of the component parts into the whole. Just as in architecture there are certain structures that cannot reveal themselves all at once, but require for their full perception a sequence of experiences linked and organized by memory, so many musical structures outdistance immediate direct perception. The *WTC*, however, is not one of these. It is simply an assemblage of spontaneous utterances, a sketchbook to which an appearance of theoretical arrangement has been given, consistent with the chronic mania for order that characterizes Bach's later years. A total performance of the *WTC*, on the one hand, is a monstrous piece of pedantry; on the other, if bearable at all, it carries an impact that a selection of individual preludes and fugues will never have as a whole, no matter how effective individually. It has some of the characteristics, at once revealing and disquieting, rich and provocative, rewarding and overwhelming, of a condensation into a single day of an eternity of experience.

Origins of Book II

Bach appears to have compiled what we now know as the second part of the *WTC* between 1739 and 1742, as indicated by the watermarks in the only surviving autograph, and to have continued revisions until 1744.[13] Bach has followed the same plan as in Book I of illustrating the possibilities of equal temperament with a prelude and fugue in each of the twenty-four major and minor tonalities. There is evidence from earlier versions that some were transposed to fit the scheme.[14] As in Book I, there is no conclusive evidence as to which

---

13. Breckoff, Werner: *Zur Entstehungsgeschichte des zweiten Wohltemperierten Klaviers von Johann Sebastian Bach*. Tübingen, 1965, p. 92.
14. Breckoff, pp. 17–24.

type of keyboard Bach might have preferred. Those who think Book II more idiomatic to the harpsichord may be faced with some very cogent evidence for its suitability to the clavichord.

Authority for calling Book II part of the *WTC* is derived from manuscript copies, of which the earliest, containing both books and known only from a later copy, bears the date 1742.[15] Other copies incorporating later revisions date from 1744 and later. The copy made in 1744 by J. C. Altnikol is entitled:

Des Wohltemperierten Claviers Zweiter Theil, bestehend in Praeludien und Fugen durch alle Tone und Semitonien, verfertigt von Johann Sebastian Bach, Königl. Pohlnisch und Churfürstl. Sächs. Hoff Compositeur Capellmeister und Directore Chori Musici in Leipzig. Im Jahre 1744.[16]

(The second part of *The Well-Tempered Clavier*, consisting of preludes and fugues in all tones and semitones, prepared by Johann Sebastian Bach, royal Polish and electoral Saxon court composer, chapelmaster and choir director in Leipzig, in the year 1744.)

No such title is borne by the autograph in the British Library in London.[17] (The Preludes and Fugues in C minor, D minor, E major, and G major, as well as the beginning of the F major Prelude, are in the hand of Anna Magdalena Bach.)[18] This manuscript did not come into public view until its acquisition by the British Museum in 1896, too late to be used by Kroll and Bischoff, the editors of the two hitherto most authoritative editions. There are two additional autographs of the A-flat Fugue in West Berlin in the Staatsbibliothek Preussischer Kulturbesitz, P274 and P213. The London autograph lacks the Preludes and Fugues in C-sharp minor, D major, and F minor.

15. Hamburg, Universitäts- und Staatsbibliothek M B/1974, Breckoff, pp. 33–34.
16. Berlin Deutsche Staatsbibliothek, Bach P 430, Breckoff, pp. 55–57.
17. British Library *Music Facsimiles I*; Johann Sebastian Bach *Das Wohltemperierte Clavier II*. Facsimile of the autograph manuscript in the British Library; Add. ms 35021; with an introduction by Don Franklin and Stephen Daw; The British Library, 1980.
18. Emery, Walter: "The London Autograph of the 'Forty Eight,'" *Music and Letters*, Vol. 34, 1953, p. 106ff.

There are more pieces of large format in Book II than in Book I, although there are comparable discrepancies of scale, created by the presence of smaller and probably earlier pieces. The disposition of the pieces in Book II, like that in Book I, obviously has no relation to an intended sequence of performance. It is a compilatory arrangement, like that of excerpts from a poet's diary or an artist's sketchbook, put in posterior order. Yet there are no duplications, and the massive, scarcely assimilable impact of the collection confronted as a whole reveals the variety and richness of its contents.

In Book II there survive more evidences of the composing process than in Book I. The Prelude in C major exists in three different versions, of which the autograph gives the second, but not the one that is commonly accepted as the final version, which can be dated 1742 according to a later copy by Gestewicz.[19] The earliest version gives a much shorter reading both of the Prelude and of the Fugue. Early versions also exist of the Preludes and Fugues in C-sharp major (originally in C major) and in D minor; of the Prelude in E-flat (originally in D); and of the Fugues in G major and A-flat major (originally in F major).[20] These are also mainly shorter versions, truncated at the ends or lacking the figural elaborations that appear in the final texts. The earlier notation in C major of what became the Prelude and Fugue in C-sharp major shows that Bach transposed the piece for the purposes of his collection. There is considerable probability that he also transposed the C-sharp minor Fugue. The Fugue in A-flat is known in an earlier abbreviated version in F major, with a completely different Prelude which is also in F major. Furthermore, for an earlier version of the G major Fugue there exist two different Preludes. (For what promises to be a definitive account of the origins and sources of the *WTC*, as well as what promises to be the first really satisfactory text, one looks forward to the forthcoming volumes of the *Neue Bach Ausgabe*, and their accompanying text revisions.)

Much that is really idiomatic to the keyboard appears in many of the preludes and in some of the fugues, but much is designed to stimulate the imagination to desert the confines of the keyboard for

19. Hamburg, Universitäts- und Staatsbibliothek, M B/1974, Breckoff, p. 67.
20. Breckoff, pp. 17–24, 66–83.

other media and for the larger dimensions of polyphonic orchestra and choir. Some pieces are sketches for jeweled miniatures, some for vast frescos. Some are intimate and lyrical; some quiver with the intensity of a passion that is just as intensely controlled; some fringe on the pedantic; and some are frankly sublime.

Part of their fascination resides in the many possible perspectives from which they can be viewed, and in the manifold aspects they can assume. What seemed schematic may reveal new freshness; what seemed dull emerges as merely misunderstood; what seemed limited displays new dimensions; to what by its very richness and concentration has become indigestible, we return after days, months, or even years, to receive new and unanticipated nourishment and revelation. One may occasionally lay aside the *WTC*, but never because of its exhaustibility.

Editions

Like all the keyboard works of Bach except the *Clavier-Übung*, the Schübler chorales, and the Canonic Variations, the *WTC* as a whole remained unpublished until a half century after Bach's death. Were it not for the existence of numerous copies, it might never have survived. Only a few separate pieces were brought out before the end of the century. In 1773 Kirnberger[21] published the A minor Prelude from Book II and the B minor Fugue from Book I, along with a thorough harmonic analysis. Reichardt[22] brought out the F minor Fugue of Book II in 1782, and Kollman[23] printed the C major Prelude and Fugue of Book II in London in 1799. The first three complete editions of the forty-eight preludes and fugues appeared all at about the same time (c. 1800–1801).[24] They were followed in the next half century by an ever-increasing number of editions among which I will mention only that of Czerny in 1837. To this very day this has probably been the most widely reprinted edition.

Of the editions which appeared after 1850, I will mention only the

21. Kirnberger, J. P.: *Die Wahren Grundsätze zum Gebrauch der Harmonie.* Berlin & Königsberg, 1773.
22. Reichardt, J. F.: *Musikalisches Kunstmagazin*, Vol. I, Berlin, 1782.
23. Kollman, A. F. C.: *Essay on Practical Musical Composition.* London, 1799.
24. Hoffmeister, Leipzig; Simrock, Bonn & Paris; Nägeli, Zürich.

important ones that still exert an influence in our own time. In 1862
Franz Kroll made his first edition of the *WTC*, which is still available
from Peters. He followed it with a wholly admirable edition for volume XIV of the Bachgesellschaft, with a preface dated 1866. Like
the biographical work of Spitta, this edition has hardly been sur-
passed. Whenever I return to it I am filled with admiration for the
thoroughness and good sense which it represents. Material supple-
mentary to Kroll's edition turns up in volumes XXXVI and XLV of
the Bachgesellschaft. In 1883 and 1884 Hans Bischoff did an independent and fresh revision of the text,[25] profiting by access to a
certain number of manuscripts that had not been available to Kroll.
Unlike Kroll in his edition for the Bachgesellschaft, however, Bischoff added fingerings and indications for dynamics, articulation, and
tempo.

It is scarcely believable that for nearly eighty years after Bischoff's
edition, no serious independent reevaluation of the text of the *WTC*
took place. Only in 1960 did East-German Peters begin publishing
an edition by Alfred Kreutz, who had already made an excellent
edition of the English Suites. After completing Book I, however,
Kreutz died, and Book II, published in 1961, was taken over by
Hermann Keller. One's hopes for a trustworthy and definitive exposition and consolidation of the manuscript material that had not been
available to Kroll and Bischoff were badly disappointed. In the case
of Book II, this is particularly regrettable, since no one has seriously
edited its text since the rediscovery of the London autograph. (Kroll's
instinct in making his selection of texts was, however, remarkably
good and his version is not as drastically upset by the readings of
the London autograph as one might expect.)

A facsimile edition of the autograph of Book I was published in
1962.[26] More recently the autograph of Book II has also been published in facsimile.[27] But it is still impossible as of 1983 to obtain

25. Bach, J. S.: *Clavierwerke, Fünfter [Sechster] Band, Kritische Ausgabe mit Fingersatz und Vortragsbezeichnungen versehen von Dr. Hans Bischoff*. Leipzig,
Steingräber [preface dated 1884]. Reprinted with notes in translation, New York,
Kalmus.
26. *Faksimile-Reihe Bachscher Werke und Shriftstücke Herausgegeben vom Bach-
Archiv Leipzig Band 5* . . . VEB Deutscher Verlag Für Musik, Leipzig, 1962.
27. British Library *Music Facsimiles I* . . . London, British Library, 1980.

from any single publication a complete panorama of the source material or a completely definitive and authoritative text. In the meantime, a survey of what is known up to now can best be achieved by using the three volumes of the Bachgesellschaft that contain Kroll's edition and the supplements to it. Reprinted in the Lea Pocket Scores series, the Bachgesellschaft edition is by far the best text, not only for choice of readings but also for clarity of engraving, avoidance of page turns, and intelligibility of voice-leading. Kroll's earlier edition for Peters is not as conclusive as his Bachgesellschaft work. Other alternatives are Bischoff, the Kreutz-Keller edition, and an edition by Otto von Irmer published by Henle, which, like the Kreutz-Keller edition, is one of those self-styled Urtext editions that nevertheless adds fingerings and, in the case of the Irmer edition, omits any accounting for its text.

Bach's Text

Bach's text of the *WTC* contains few directions for the performer. Indications of articulation are exceedingly sparse, confined almost entirely to a few staccato marks and to a few slurs that seldom embrace more than two notes. There are two fugue subjects that have interesting slurring, namely the B-flat in Book II and the B minor in Book I. The only indication of dynamics in the entire *WTC* occurs in the echo effects of the Prelude in G-sharp minor of Book II. For the most part ornamentation is incompletely and inexactly notated. I think there is no possibility of saying that the ornamentation in the *WTC* represents a definitive aspect of the text.

Early and Later Fashions in Playing Bach

Most accounts of Bach's own keyboard playing date from a generation later and do not tell us very much about his handling of the instrument that is reliable. As usual for performers of his day, many accounts speak of his improvisation more than of his style of playing. Most evident, however, are his innovations in the scope of keyboard technique merely in the note-negotiating sense. Most of the great keyboard composers of the seventeenth and eighteenth centuries were far from having the kind of universal keyboard technique that became common in the nineteenth and twentieth centuries. They were equipped to play the music of their own style and of their own school and very little else. The relative universality of Bach's approach to the keyboard reflects his inveterate eclecticism.

Fashions in Bach performance have changed radically and often since Bach's time. About the generation immediately following, we have very little information, but it begins to emerge with the first publications of Bach keyboard works in the early nineteenth century and with Forkel's biography in 1802.[28] A style of playing distinctly oriented to the clavichord is expounded in Griepenkerl's edition of the *Chromatic Fantasy* in 1819.[29] This results from Forkel's identification of the clavichord as Bach's preferred instrument, which probably reflects the taste of the generation after Bach more than it does the practice of Bach's own time. The Griepenkerl edition is preceded by an account of clavichord playing, presumably derived through Forkel from Bach's eldest son, Wilhelm Friedemann. The indications for performance consist of lavish espressivo dynamics, a thoroughly sensitive and pre-Romantic conception.

Another manifestation of early piano style is to be found in Czerny's much-distributed edition of *The Well-Tempered Clavier*. In his original preface of 1837, Czerny claims to transmit what he remembers of Beethoven's performances of the preludes and fugues. This sort of recollection is always to be taken with a large dose of salt. From the perspective of today I must say that I find it utterly impossible to take the Czerny edition seriously.

After the appearance of the Czerny edition in 1837 Bach becomes firmly established in the classic repertoire of the piano. Whether or not his compositions had originated as pedagogic tools, they then continued for more than a century to furnish a staple diet for willing and unwilling piano students. As instruments of either delight or torture, they became models of composition for classes in counter-

28. Forkel, J. N.: *Üeber Johann Sebastian Bachs Leben, Kunst und Kunstwerke* . . . Leipzig, 1802. Facsimile with a foreword by Ralph Kirkpatrick. New York, C. F. Peters, 1950.
29. Bach, J. S.: *Chromatische Fantasie für das Pianoforte* . . . *Neue Ausgage mit einer Bezeichnung ihres Wahren Vortrags, wie derselbe von J. S. Bach auf W. Friedemann Bach, von diesem auf Forkel und von Forkel auf seine Schüler gekommen.* Leipzig, im Bureau de Musique von C. F. Peters [1819].

point and fugue, monuments of note negotiation for beginners at the keyboard, and examples of style. (Hummel's piano method of 1828 gives the C-sharp minor Fugue from the first book as an example of legato style.)[30]

An ever-mounting wave of Bach performances was launched by Zelter's productions of cantatas and passions at the Berlin Singakademie, the famous Mendelssohn revival of the *St. Matthew Passion* in 1829, and the editions and polemics of Schumann and Robert Franz. All this activity was colored by the necessity of making Bach palatable to the nineteenth century. He was a forgotten composer who had to be championed. Often there was no question of historicism, no question of fidelity to text; the important thing was to get his music across, to make its hidden riches apparent. As a result, performers and editors made free with Bach's music and his musical style in a period of adaptation and remodeling in very much the same way that we are now busily engaged in sabotaging Richard Wagner. Despite these trends there was fortunately a conversative strain in the editorship of the Bachgesellschaft edition when its editorial policy was established in 1850. Wise decisions were made about respect for texts, and buried in the prefaces is a surprising amount of knowledge of eighteenth-century practices one would suppose to have been totally forgotten.

Bach made his way into the gradually expanding concert world, thanks to transcriptions of his organ works by Liszt and others, most notably Busoni, which to this day have never become entirely obsolete. Busoni is perhaps one of those who made freest with Bach's texts and creative ideas. Whatever legitimate disagreements they may inspire, Busoni's editions are the work of an extraordinary musical mind. There is nothing in Busoni's edition of the *WTC*,[31] whether one agrees with it or not, that has not passed through a keen ear and an alert musical sense. Its suggestions for performance and many of its basic attitudes may now be obsolete—I am not sure that we can adopt very many of them—but they do arouse in me a profound sympathy and respect.

30. Hummel, J. N.: *Ausfürhliche theoretisch-practishe Anweisung zum Piano-Forte-Spiel*, . . . Wien . . . 1828.
31. Bach, J. S.: *Klavierwerke I-II* . . . *herausgegeben von Ferruccio Busoni* . . . Leipzig, Breitkopf & Härtel [1894–1915].

Since the middle of the nineteenth century the *WTC* has achieved the status of a musical Bible. It would be very difficult to think of a major work of Western music that more fully fills a comparable function. It means something to almost everyone; that is to say that it means something different to almost everyone. It has provided an inexhaustible source of supply for keyboard practice, for the study of composition, for the exercise of students in musical analysis, and for purveyors of every conceivable kind of musical theory.

Until the present day, the conservatory tradition of Bach keyboard playing has pursued more or less an uninterrupted course. One of its later manifestations is to be seen in an edition by Bela Bartók which dates from the beginning of this century.[32] I find its approach as difficult to understand as that of Czerny, particularly when I think of the magnificent compositions of Bartók's later years and the extraordinary musical perceptiveness they show.

Along with the conservatory style and the concert transcriptions went the continuing tradition and influence of the Leipzig school, as represented to this day in the performing editions of Breitkopf and Härtel. One of the best-known and most influential representatives of the Leipzig school was Max Reger, whose edition of the A minor Triple Concerto could be cited as an almost perfect example of misunderstanding of Bach's musical language. Its scheme of dynamics and its entire system of phrasing and articulation offer a memorable lesson in how not to deal with Bach.

In their way the French organists and the English Bach choirs were keeping a Bach tradition alive, as did the annual productions of *Passionsmusik* in every German town. But at the turn of the century there began a reevaluation of the previous 150 years of what the Germans so ungracefully term *Bachpflege*. One of the earliest spokesmen of this reevaluation was Albert Schweitzer,[33] whose views on Bach performance had a wide influence, which I myself felt in my youth. If they now seem a little amateurish and outmoded, they nevertheless marked the beginning of an attempt to strip away cer-

---

32. Bach, J. S.: *Das Wohltemperierte Klavier I [II]* . . . *progressiv geordnet, neu eingerichtet, mit Fingersatz, Vortragszeichen und Anmerkungen versehen von Bartók Béla.* Zenemūkiadó Vállalat, Budapest, 1964.
33. Schweitzer, Albert: *J. S. Bach.* Leipzig, 1908.

tain accretions of the nineteenth century, to return to what seemed to be the values of Bach's own time.

About this time there began a tentative revival of obsolete instruments. A new interest in the harpsichord gradually arose following upon the experiments in the construction of modern harpsichords that began in 1888 and that were first brought before the public at the Paris Exposition of 1889. In later years the so-called Baroque organ came to be increasingly preferred over the nineteenth-century organ. More and more attention was paid to Bach's original texts and there emerged that phenomenon known as the Bach specialist.

All these tendencies of the nineteenth and early twentieth centuries are still with us, but no one could have predicted the extraordinary burgeoning of Bach's popularity, especially in the last thirty years. I can remember a time when it was still necessary to defend Bach and the performance of his music in public. Now this is clearly no longer necessary. Yet many traces of the impassioned polemic attendant upon the Bach revival of the nineteenth century survive in the vehemence of the doctrines of present-day Bach specialists. Indeed, so many views are changing today that a fairly complete re-evaluation may take place over the next twenty or thirty years. What turn it will take remains to be seen.

A New Search for Bach

Since my approach throughout this book is directed more toward those elements in the *WTC* that are timeless, rather than those that might seem to demand a certain amount of historicity, I shall pass rather lightly over much of what generally concerns many a player of early music and especially over those considerations of authenticity which may seem to oppose or even threaten to dominate those of artistry.

All too often a necessarily incomplete and misunderstood historicism has been applied to those elements which are most perishable in that music and which confine it to the peculiarities of its own time and to the limitations of the historian's own perceptions. While respecting the considerable body of historical information which has helped us to correct, or at least to modify, the prejudices and misconceptions of the generations immediately preceding our own, I wish to concentrate on those qualities which make good music timeless, and on the inner life in that music which constantly permits new insights and reevaluations and which permits it to speak in its own terms to persons and to cultures that may be far removed in both time and distance from its origins.

Although I attach considerable importance to the use of historical fingerings in the works of such composers as William Byrd and Couperin and their contemporaries, I take no interest whatever in the attempt to reconstruct historical fingerings in the playing of such highly unidiomatic keyboard music as that of J. S. Bach. The only examples of fingering written down by Bach himself are to be found in the little "Applicatio" that begins the *Clavier-Büchlein vor Wilhelm Friedemann Bach* and in the G minor Praeambulum in the same book[34]. The earliest version of the C-major Prelude and Fugue in Book II is known in a manuscript copy by J. P. Kellner, containing fairly complete fingerings.[35] Otherwise we have very little evidence of Bach's own fingering except by deduction from instruction books and occasional manuscripts by other composers.

Bach can be said to have straddled the transition between ancient and modern fingering. The ancient fingering was based upon a crossing of a longer finger over a shorter. In other words, the ascending C major scale in the right hand was executed one two three four, three four, etc.; and five four three two, three two, etc., in descending. The principle of what the French call the *passage du pouce* had not been discovered, except in a rudimentary fashion in the fingering for the left hand. One ascended the scale five four three two one two, one two etc.; and descended one two three four, three four, three four five. The only example of fingering directly pertinent to the *WTC* is to be found in the above-mentioned manuscript copy of an early version of the C major Prelude and Fugue of Book II. While in the past I felt obliged to respect it, I can now regard it as a thoroughly bad fingering.

---

34. Bach, J. S.: *Clavier-Büchlein vor Wilhelm Friedemann Bach*, edited in facsimile with a preface by Ralph Kirkpatrick. New Haven, Yale University Press, 1959, p. 9 and p. 20.

35. Staatsbibliothek Preussischer Kulturbesitz Mus. Ms. P. 804, pp. 235, 238–239. First printed in BG XXXVI, pp. 224–225.

Example 1.1 Prelude C-sharp minor, II

The signs for ornamentation in the *WTC* are neither complete nor necessarily definitive (Example 1.1), aside from the fact that even where indicated nearly all of Bach's ornamentation requires supplementing.[36] A study of parallel passages in Bach's ornamentation reveals the latitude afforded the player in adding trills to descending appoggiaturas or in adding prefixes and suffixes to trills even where not expressly indicated, or in converting the first auxiliary note of a trill into an appoggiatura like that of the *Tremblement appuyé* of the French. Likewise a mordent can be added to a grace note from below in terms of the French *Port-de-voix et pincé*. Thus in Example 1.2 the addition of trills and mordents to passages where only ap-

---

36. Hermann Keller's notes on ornamentation in the beginning of his edition of Book II of the *WTC* [Leipzig, Peters] are too perfunctory to merit credibility.

Example 1.2 Prelude C-sharp minor, II, with added ornaments

poggiaturas are indicated reveals the possibility of rendering more flexible the somewhat doctrinaire prescriptions of C. P. E. Bach's *Versuch* and of later treatises concerning the length of appoggiaturas. I have indicated the value I have assigned to certain grace notes or appoggiaturas in small notes above or below the ornament in question. Certain ornaments can sometimes be suppressed in terms of the general context, like the one in Example 1.1 which I have enclosed in parentheses. While this example is taken from my harpsichord recording, the clavichord recording is slightly different.

I cannot think of a single piece in the *WTC* even among those in which no signs for ornaments appear to which ornamentation might not conceivably be added. But in adding ornamentation for which there is no authorization in Bach's text, the player is likely to risk defacing rather than enhancing the beauty of Bach's own simpler part-writing. All too frequently ornamentations introduced by players whose taste and skill are not comparable to Bach's merely resemble the bird droppings that disfigure the statues of great men. Bach's ornamentation reflects a transition period. Prior to the end of Bach's life, German keyboard treatises were quite as rare as was any really systematic codification of ornamentation. But from 1750 to the end of the century there appeared a spate of highly articulate and well-organized German treatises which dealt with ornamentation. It can be argued that my discussion of Bach ornamentation in my 1938 edition of the Goldberg Variations (New York, G. Schirmer) was excessively restricted by the prescriptions of the treatises on which I based it.[37] There are, however, certain practices that would appear to have been quite logical, but for which these treatises give insufficient concrete evidence. I am referring to certain kinds of short appoggiaturas, anticipations of ornaments, and beginnings of trills from below. All of these are ruled out by the majority of the later treatises. My own preferences, at least those of the 1960s, can be ascertained from my recordings of the WTC. (In the case of the Goldberg Variations my latest performances substituted short grace notes for many of the long appoggiaturas that were written out in my edition and all modifications of the written text in terms of double dotting were eliminated entirely.) The most recent and the most exhaustive, although not wholly unbiased, survey of the sources is given in a monumental work by Frederick Neumann.[38]

It has always seemed to me that many discussions of ornamentation, both ancient and modern, fail to take into consideration the important differentiations available to the player, depending on whether or not the accentuation at the beginning of an ornament is thrown onto the note it decorates (thus a short grace note can be played as a grace note on the beat represented by the main note), or onto the main note itself in a manner which can almost and sometimes actu-

37. Alfred Kreutz in the *Beilage* to his edition of the English Suites [Leipzig, Peters] and Georg von Dadelsen in his article "Verzierungen" in *Die Musik in Geschichte und Gegenwart* offer lucid and reasonably objective expositions of what might be termed the classic view of ornamentation as based on eighteenth-century treatises.

38. Neumann, Frederick: *Ornamentation in Baroque and Post-Baroque Music with special emphasis on J. S. Bach.* Princeton, 1978.

ally does sound as if the ornament were being anticipated or, in other words, played before the beat. The question of beginning trills with the upper or the lower note is completely subsidiary in my view to the question of whether or not the accentuation is thrown onto the auxiliary or onto the main note. For example, the trill which begins the subject of the F-sharp major Fugue of Book II or the sustained trills of the Prelude in G minor of Book I can each be played in such a manner that although the trill actually begins with the upper auxiliary note, the listener's attention is focused on the main note. In my view it is not absolutely necessary, as some have assumed, to begin such trills with a main note. If at the opening of the C minor two-part Invention the short trill in measure 3, though begun on the upper auxiliary, is played in such a way as to focus the attention on the dissonance created by the main note G against the A-flat in the bass, there is no need to fear that the player will be disturbed by the parallel octaves in such fashion as to feel obliged to play what later was called an inverted mordent by beginning the trill on the main note. (Example 1.3)

Example 1.3 Invention 2

For many years there was an avowed theoretical connection between a time signature and a tempo. This connection had largely broken down in Bach's day and any attempt to deduce categories of tempo or character of performance from his time signatures is a debatable operation. The metric units in which a piece from the *WTC* is notated are more likely to indicate differences of character than of actual tempo. Certainly the eighteenth-century French manner of beating meters notated in units of three eighth notes in terms of two unequal beats on notes one and three as differentiated from the prevailing manner of beating triple units notated in quarter notes in terms of three equal beats may well have exerted a strong influence.[39] There is much, I think, that has been intimated by the choice of note values, but I question whether the evidence is sufficient to permit the formation of any doctrine. The existence of the B minor Prelude of Book II in two versions,[40] one of which gives notes of half the value of the commonly known text, is enough to discredit any too assiduous attempt to associate note values and tempo.

Rhythmic questions, such as the treatment of dotted notes and of dotted notes against triplets, arise in a few pieces of the *WTC*, but always in the context of a decorated characterization of simpler subject material. I see no binding historical evidence that would authorize their being played otherwise than as they are notated, with the exception of the F-sharp major Prelude of Book II which embodies the characteristic eighteenth-century shortcut in notation showing a dotted eighth followed by three thirty-second notes instead of resorting to a second dot or a tied-over thirty-second note. Little that has been written about conventional alterations of rhythm in eighteenth-century music seems to have much bearing on the *WTC*. To invoke a blanket "rule" prescribing assimilation into triplet movement of dotted notes or even eighth notes accompanied by triplets (as has been done) would in my view render the subject of the E minor Fugue of Book II quite as preposterous (Example 1.4) as would a comparable treatment in some "authentic" performance some centuries hence of the following measures of the Liszt B Minor Sonata (Example 1.5). A timely refutation of the now widespread practice of double dotting in eighteenth-century music is to be found in Frederick Neumann's article, "The Over-Dotting Syndrome: Anatomy of a Delusion."[41]

---

39. The greater importance of differentiation of character rather than of actual speed was less apparent to me than it is now when I published my article "Eighteenth-Century Metronomic Indications" in *Papers Read by Members of the American Musicological Society at the Annual Meeting*, Washington, D.C., 1938.
40. See BG XIV, p. 270.
41. Neumann, Frederick: "The Over-Dotting Syndrome: Anatomy of a Delusion," *Musical Quarterly*, Vol. 67 (1981), pp. 305–347. Reprinted in Frederick Neumann's *Essays in Performance Practice*. Ann Arbor, UMI Research Press, 1982.

Example 1.4 Fugue E minor, II, rewritten

Example 1.5 Liszt, B minor Sonata, rewritten

As an interpreter, I have an overwhelming predilection for making the most direct contact possible with a composer or a composer's text. I am unwilling to tolerate the presence of an intermediary, whether it be an editor or another interpreter. Obviously this attitude will work only for the performer who is calling the tune. It will not do much for the orchestral player. My point of view is primarily that of the independent, free-searching individual. It is understandable that many ensemble players and orchestral players seldom indulge in ideas and convictions of their own. Subject as they are to the tyranny of good and bad conductors and to all sorts of compromise, the constant frustration would be too painful. Superb ensemble players often exhibit a notable reluctance to engage in theory and a certain pride in never having looked at the footnotes to a text. This method of self-protection gets them through their long hours of rehearsals with a minimum of anguish. But for those of us who are relatively free to exercise our sensibilities and convictions—especially teachers, who must treasure that freedom—the individualistic approach is absolutely necessary.

One can now find out a great deal about so-called performance practice contemporary with Bach. When I began playing, traditions of dynamics, phrasing, and ornamentation were much less common knowledge than they have since become. The revival of certain eighteenth-century practices may well become so widespread that the kind of scholarship necessary in my generation will no longer need to be pursued so intensively. But I cannot abandon a conviction that a conscientious interpreter of the music of the past has an obligation to know as much as he possibly can about the way in which that music was conceived by its composer and performed by his contemporaries, however much he may decide to depart from this necessarily insufficient body of knowledge. The same can be said for the choice of instruments: when to use obsolete instruments, when to replace them, how to choose instruments when they are not specified, how strongly to reinforce a vocal or instrumental ensemble to suit the performing conditions of our time.

All of this brings us up against Pilate's question, What is historical truth? If it is possible to know it, how valuable is it to us in the domain of art? It is quite clear that even if we have fulfilled our obligation to know as much as we can about the historical background of Bach's music, that knowledge is far from sufficient to permit a working program. Even if we were content with it, it would have to be supplemented with a vast amount of conjecture, and the question always arises whether, in works of art, the source offers the very last word.

Is not what has subsequently sprung from that source, that which has happened since, of comparable importance? Can any good piece of music be taken as a definitive statement once and for all? Is it not more true to say that it has manifold implications, infinite possibilities of meaning and counterbalance, so that it demands, just as does any fascinating human being, constant reinterpretation? If this were not the case, it would probably be dead. In history, is it what actually happened that counts, or is it what the next generation thought had happened? I think in many cases one can say that our attitudes toward historical events are more important than the events themselves.

Suppose that, in our veneration for the source and our search for historical verities, we managed to unearth a tape recording of Bach's performance of his keyboard works. Would we like what we heard?

I wonder. Because composers are primarily concerned with getting the right combinations of notes on paper, they may have a certain justifiable indifference to establishing communication with mere listeners. Would we find Bach's keyboard performances pedestrian, as we often do poets' readings of their own poetry? Or would these performances stop us dead in our tracks, make us henceforth cease to perform, lest we diminish with our trivial version the definitive word from Mt. Sinai? Since we have never kept very well to the original words from Mt. Sinai, I suppose much the same fate would greet the performance of Bach.

Literature about *The Well-Tempered Clavier*

Not all of the literature about the *WTC* arouses trust. In fact, one might measure the significance of a work of art by the amount of nonsense that it is capable of generating. In terms of having inspired abundant nonsense, the *WTC* achieves a fairly high place, even though the total amount of writing about it is not as great as one might have expected. The shortcomings of much of this writing are often due to a desire on the part of authors to prove rather than to perceive. One may easily be brought to the conclusion that the best book on the *WTC* is the *WTC* itself in a critical Urtext edition like that of Kroll (BG XIV) or in the worthy successor to it that is still to be awaited.

In the numerous works analyzing the preludes and fugues, there is very little that I have actually read. While exception might well be taken to my lack of interest in most of this analytical writing, I may as well confess it nevertheless. Analytical theory in relation to performance needs to be digestible in simple concepts that have to do with direct experience. I cannot undertake to eat what I cannot assimilate. Most analytical studies are of little use to me as an interpreter, including that grisly chapter of my own that I entitled "The Anatomy of the Scarlatti Sonata."[42] Many a comparable study might well bear the title "The Autopsy of the Bach Fugue."

Formal analysis serves to orient, yet it cannot produce experience but can only chart it. A distinction should be made between the kind of analysis which closes the ears and that which opens them. It is all

---

42. Kirkpatrick, Ralph: *Domenico Scarlatti*. Princeton, 1953.

too frequent that analyses are accepted at face value. Very often the procedures leading to such analyses may have been quite fruitful and rewarding for the author. But no author can do a reader's hearing for him, and when the results of an analysis are approached by a reader who has not followed through the operations that led to them, the analysis is more likely to deaden than to quicken sensibilities. But certainly no technique which obliges anyone to look or listen can be entirely useless.

In relation to direct confrontation with the work at hand, historical information is useful, but certainly not sufficient. Thirty years ago I was much more interested in the historical approach than I am now. It would now be very difficult for me to agree to teach a course in performance practice, because I think that it has now become all too easy to regard certain perennial unanswered and unanswerable questions as already answered by the documents of history. One cannot sidestep artistic and interpretive problems by relegating them to the dictates of historical authority. Ways of supplementing historical authority are what, after the preliminaries of these first two chapters, I propose that we examine.

CHAPTER II.

The Esthetic Approach

The Pieces of *The Well-Tempered Clavier*

With the term *esthetic approach* I have made rather free. Originally it was designed to provide some sort of convenient distinction from what I called the interpretative approach. The latter presupposes a commitment on the part of the interpreter that the observer, no matter how deeply he may feel, is not obliged to make. Whether right or wrong, an interpreter is committed from the minute he sits down at an instrument. The observer makes his approach from outside, so to speak, the interpreter from inside. The levels on which one approaches the music are determined by the purpose one has in mind. The listener has a level of understanding that is perhaps fortunately free of any necessity for verbalization. The commentator, regardless of how well he may or may not have listened, has sooner or later to decide what he is going to say. The composer is likely to be attentive to the way in which the piece is made, and the performer to the way in which it is to be played.

The term *prelude* is very seldom applied to anything but a piece to be dealt with by a solo performer. The exceptions to this rule are so few as to be almost negligible. Throughout its history the prelude is founded on an extemporized series of chords with varying degrees of formal organization and decoration. The unmeasured preludes of the French seventeenth-century *clavecinist* are only partially no-

32

tated. Rhythmic values are not indicated and durations only sketched in. Perhaps more than documents or compositions, they are indications of how one might improvise preludes. In the history of pieces called preludes we find a continuous process of elaboration. More and more, preludes become set pieces, big constructions carefully disciplined and highly organized. This history reflects itself in a progression that can be established through the preludes of the *WTC*.

Thus we may go from the arpeggiated simple chords of the first prelude of Book I through a consistent pattern of figuration, as in C minor I, continuo chords with superposed melody (E minor I), the continuo skeleton with even more sophisticated melodic figuration (F minor I), the two-part invention with double counterpoint (C-sharp major I), the three-part sinfonia (A major II, and B-flat minor II), excursions into the fugal style (E-flat I, and C-sharp major II), and toccata style (B-flat major I). Binary invention forms make their appearance (D-sharp minor II, E minor II, and A minor II), and in Book II certain forms are given a ternary feeling by the return toward the end of initial thematic material (E-flat major II, and F-sharp minor II).

The progression from the simple to the complex is the most illuminating way in which one can look at the music of Bach. Bach is always working outward from the harmonic tonal skeleton, and imposing layers of melodic and contrapuntal decoration on it. Bach nearly always elaborates and almost never simplifies. This perhaps accounts for the fact that his style fell out of fashion at the end of his life, when nothing was more prized than an elegant and chaste simplicity.

Fugues run from two to five voices, simple, double, triple, with a variety of strettos, inversions, and episodes. Their tonal structure varies and a few of them even approach binary form, as in C major, D minor, and F minor in Book I. There are fugues whose melodic configurations mark them as instrumental fugues clearly related to Bach's orchestral treatment of similar material. There are also the predominantly vocal fugues that recall the *stile antico* of the choral music of preceding centuries (C-sharp minor, D-sharp minor, B-flat minor in Book I, and E-flat major and E major in Book II). Some fugues seem to be less orthodox, more experimental, than others.

The Italian eighteenth-century fugue from which stems a great deal of later fugue writing is a totally different thing from the Bach fugue. It is much more a manner than a style. Rather than an organic assemblage of forms, it resembles the plastering on of a facade. It is like a great deal of Italian Renaissance and Baroque architecture in the sense that the visual organization goes no deeper than the walls of Roman brick behind the stucco and marble of the surface decoration. And this I think accounts for the lack of interest that one is likely to take in a fugue of one of the Scarlatti family or of Padre Martini or any of their followers, compared with the fugues of Bach himself. The Classical fugues, the post-Bach fugues, of Mozart and Beethoven are much more in the Italian tradition than in the Bach tradition, even when their composers think they are paying homage to Bach.

The fugue can hardly be called a natural phenomenon. I find myself defining it as an unnatural structure composed of natural elements. It is fully as unnatural as the clipped boxwood garden of the eighteenth century or the five positions of classical ballet. It is as unnatural as the arbitrary rules set up for all sorts of games, unless one holds the view that all of this reflects in a dim way a higher discipline of some sort.

Any attempt at classification of pieces of the *WTC* in terms of common features will reveal that every piece on close inspection shows a character fundamentally different from every other. There are no duplications in the *WTC*. Nor can one find such a thing as a typical fugue. After I had analyzed and attempted to classify some five hundred Scarlatti sonatas, I came to the conclusion that it was impossible to find a single example of what might be cited as a typical Scarlatti sonata; I had to make up one. In like fashion, if one wants to find a typical Bach fugue, one has to fabricate it. The result of this fabrication will be nothing other than what we know as a school fugue. It is like those models that are constructed to demonstrate human anatomy, a wooden image of a fugue. Diversity, evidently, is appreciable only in relation to uniformity.

Organization of the *WTC*

One may ask whether there is any relationship between one piece and another in the *WTC*. What, for example, is the relation between prelude and fugue or, in collective terms, between preludes and fugues? Certainly any such relationship can be one of contrast or of complement. The complementary relationship of a prelude leading to a fugue is often underlined, as in the members of a pair of Scarlatti sonatas, by a similarity of instrumental character, by a kind of imaginary instrumentation for the same orchestra or for the same group of players. There have been numerous rather debatable attempts to point out thematic relationships between preludes and fugues, like those by Johann Nepomuk David,[1] and even by Busoni.[2] However, there are quite as many preludes that contrast violently with the fugues that they precede. They seem designed not to introduce the fugue but to set it off.

The transition from one prelude and fugue to another is sometimes quite smooth, but at other times it can be disconcertingly abrupt. Perhaps in Book I the two great five-voice fugues are intentionally placed at what might be called centers of gravity. Perhaps Bach did attempt to make some kind of balanced distribution of the various pieces. But whether this has anything to do with an arrangement for performance is questionable.

A discovery that has doubtless been made before flashed into my consciousness one morning before a complete performance of Book I. Meditating on the peculiarities of the B minor Fugue and on the discrepancy between the expository material and the episodes, I suddenly realized that the subject includes all twelve notes of the chromatic scale. I then looked for correspondences elsewhere in Book I, and counted off the notes represented in the twelfth fugue, the F minor. There I also found the twelve tones of the chromatic scale, not in the subject alone, but in the combined subject and answer. It is noteworthy that these two fugues mark the middle and the end of Book I. (But subsequent meditation has not enabled me to claim J. S. Bach as a twelve-tone composer!) Perhaps some future analysis of the *WTC*, preferably in which wishful thinking is outweighed by integrity and common sense, will be able to contribute further to an understanding of its organization.

1. David, J. N.: *Das Wohltemperierte Klavier, Das Versuch einer Synopsis.* Göttingen, 1962.
2. Bach, J. S.: *Klavierwerke I-II . . . herausgegeben von Ferruccio Busoni . . .* Leipzig [1894–1915].

The most satisfactory conclusion to which one can come about the organization of the preludes and fugues is simply that there is at least a principle of avoiding monotony in their sequence and providing variety in their distribution. One is tempted to look for an organizing principle beyond that of sequence and distribution, but as far as I know no one can be trusted to have found it. Other large pieces, at least the Goldberg Variations, the organ *Clavier-Übung*, the B minor Mass, and to a certain extent the Passions, exhibit a span that transcends the effect of individual movements or of their arrangement. In such pieces, smaller movements are incorporated into a larger form, and the sequence of movements is obviously designed for dramatic effect as well as for formal coherence. The question poses itself: Does the *WTC* have any real existence as an artistic construction? Or is it merely a posteriorly organized collection of pieces of relatively haphazard origin? Clearly it has no resemblance to a work like the B minor Mass, which despite its having been made up for the most part of pieces that were originally written for other purposes achieves a high degree of formal and dramatic construction.

In the succession of pieces in the *WTC*, there are a few effective transitions, but there is much that would appear to be anticlimactic. It is very difficult to arrange the grouping of pieces so that in a performance of the *WTC* as a whole something can emerge that resembles a well-made concert program. There is no appreciable dramatic progression or symmetry. As for the role of different tonalities in the *WTC*, however much they may have influenced the character and treatment of individual pieces, there is no trace of an overall scheme such as a later composer might have used in order to tie all the twenty-four tonalities together, as did Chopin in his remarkably successful arrangement of the Preludes.

Given the variety of pieces in the *WTC* and the avoidance of duplication, it is conceivable that Bach was deliberately exploiting the scope of his expressive possibilities. Could this possibly have been Bach's *Traité des passions*? If so, I can find no evidence of a systematic marshalling of the emotions that Bach's contemporaries and the theorists of the *Affektenlehre* considered expressible in music. Certainly many of the individual pieces of the *WTC* partake so clearly of the same characteristics as their vocal counterparts in the cantatas and Passions that one has little difficulty in predicting, at least roughly, what kind of text any given piece in the *WTC* might have had. It would have been quite normal for him to try to run the gamut of all possible emotions in a classification similar to those that so often appear in philosophical and poetical works of the seventeenth and eighteenth centuries. Although I have found no evidence of such a systematic approach, others have been more industrious.

One author has painstakingly set up the whole of Book II as a scenario for the principal happenings of the Old and New Testaments.[3] Measures have been counted, and the component notes of fugue subjects added up to demonstrate all sorts of occult correspondences. Almost every unit of three is taken to refer to the Trinity, and any half dozen must necessarily be considered to allude to the six days of Creation. It is true that in Bach's vocal works deliberate symbolism has been proved beyond any doubt, even to the number eleven as alluding to the twelve Apostles minus Judas. We therefore cannot entirely dismiss every hypothesis of symbolism in the *WTC* as the dream of a crackpot. But no one with any comprehension of Bach's habit of imposing various levels of decoration on simple forms can take seriously any numerological symbolism that is based on a mere counting of notes.

The only organizing principle that I can attribute with any security to the *WTC* as a whole is the following, namely, that two sets of twenty-four preludes and fugues, none of which resembles another, have been assembled in the chromatic order of the twelve major and minor degrees of the tempered scale. This is of course nothing other than what Bach explicitly states in his title.

Why did Bach write the *WTC* at all? As a consummate improviser, accustomed daily to turning out all but perhaps the very strictest fugues, he probably attached little importance to the writing down of keyboard music for his own use. Certainly neither he nor other keyboard players needed vehicles for concert performances. He had few illusions about the chances of publication. In assembling the *WTC* he was probably doing exactly what his title page declares, furnishing a model of composition, showing how it should and could be done, providing instruction for beginners and pleasure for profes-

---

3. Nissen, Hans: "Der Sinn des 'Wohltemperierten Klaviers II. Teil,'" *Bach-Jahrbuch*, Vol. 39 [1951–1952], pp. 54–80.

sionals. Of performance as definitive, as an end in itself, he probably hardly thought. This is perhaps one of the reasons why so many questions of instrumental designation, of ornamentation, of dynamics, of timbre, and even of phrasing and articulation are left unanswered. This is why it is unwise to attribute to Bach himself many of the decisions, or the specific orientations, and the narrowing down of possibilities that everyone who plays the *WTC* must undertake. Bach himself would have been in command of so many resources, even those of substituting totally different pieces, that many of the problems with which performers must necessarily plague themselves would have shrunk in his consciousness to total insignificance.

If, then, the *WTC* is only a posteriorly organized collection of separate older and newer pieces, what is its fascination as a whole? Why are we drawn to considering the preludes and fugues in relation to each other? Is it merely habit, because they are bound in the same two volumes? Is it a collective expression of the lifelong love and admiration we have felt for these pieces? Or is it merely a feeling that everything throws light on everything else? Perhaps that unconscious unity which pervades the *WTC* is simply a reflection of the unity which emanates from Bach's personality. It is a unity that has elevated many a set of diaries or letters into literature, and sketches into art. It perhaps derives from the fact that for Bach the musical language was as complete and unquestionable as the theological system. In exploring and exploiting the utmost resources of that tonal system he achieved a voyage through his own musical universe that has much in common with those we have the privilege of knowing about from a few poets, philsophers, and prophets.

The *WTC* and Instrumental Sound

In many ways the *WTC* is the most impractical, the least idiomatic of Bach's keyboard works. It is only with an occasional prelude that one arrives at something that makes the harpsichord sound as well as in a sonata of Scarlatti or a piece of Couperin or Rameau. It is even a little disconcerting when certain pieces of the *WTC* leap out from the prevailing tone of austerity and restraint. These are the moments when for once one can stop the effort of imagining an ideal music and simply listen to the actual sound produced by the instru-

Example 2.1 Handel, Suite IV in E minor, Allegro, from Pasquali

ment. Most standard keyboard literature is written fundamentally in
two voices, whether or not supplied with harmonic filling. Only with
a certain effort does one apprehend more than the two outer parts in
keyboard music.

In a treatise by Nicolo Pasquali[4] entitled *The Art of Fingering the
Harpsichord* appears the following passage headed "Objections against
playing Fugues in three or four Parts on the harpsichord":

> This is a Kind of playing, that forty Years ago was much more
> in Vogue than at present; but, as it has still some Partizans, it is
> necessary here to examine its Nature, in order to form a Judg-
> ment, whether it is fit for a Harpsichord or not.
>
>   . . . many Passages in Fugues and other Compositions in three
> or four Parts, cannot be played on the Harpsichord, neither as
> they are written, nor with a good Tone. And as a Proof of this
> Assertion, let us observe Part of the Fugue in the fourth suit of
> Mr. HANDEL's first Set of Lessons . . . beginning at the thirty-
> second Bar [Example 2.1]; in which we shall find not only that

---

4. Pasquali, Nicolo: *The Art of Fingering the Harpsichord* . . . London [*c.* 1765.
    An earlier edition was published in Edinburgh *c.* 1758].

it is impossible to hold every Note its full Length, according to the past Rules, as it does not admit of a Regularity of Fingers; but also by the too great Nearness of the Parts, the Ear will confound the Passages of one Part with those of another, and often reduce the Effect of four Parts to that of two. And when it so happens, that the Musick is so much interwoven, that the Ear cannot reduce it to two Parts, then it has often the Effect of mere Thorough-bass. [What Pasquali would have said forty years later on the first English publication of the fugues of the *Well-Tempered Clavier* can be imagined.]

Many Musick-masters have never thought of this Defect, because while they play, or hear a Fugue played, they generally look upon the Book, and their Imagination fills up all the Deficiencies of the Performance: But it is not so with the unskilled Person that hears it at a Distance; for such a one has nothing to listen to but the Effect, and when that is defective, then he must be displeased rather than entertained.

He analyzes his example from Handel and concludes:

Upon the Whole, I really believe, that Passages with complicated Parts in the Manner above-mentioned, are not natural for the Instrument, and therefore ought to be avoided as much as possible; witness Mr. *Handel's* Conduct in this Particular: For when he composed the above quoted Suits of Lessons, he was a young Man, and, in all probability, followed the then reigning Taste in his Compositions, without reflecting any further; but when Experience shewed him the true Power of the Harpsichord, in a maturer Time of Life, he published his celebrated first six Concertos for the Organ or Harpsichord; in which it is worth observing, that he has put only one Fugue amongst them all; though he is, in my Opinion, one of the best Composers of Fugues that ever existed. . . .

He remarks that all the rest of the concertos are composed only in two parts. I think one could find many reasons for agreeing with Pasquali that, viewed from a certain aspect, the keyboard fugue is one of the greatest monstrosities that has ever been invented. It is indeed, as he says, a challenge to the imagination. He perhaps forgets that the imagination delights in such challenges and that there are many other forms of art which are fully based on them.

Legend has it in our own time that the harpsichord is particularly suited for playing fugues and contrapuntal music in general. I do not think that this is any more true than Pasquali thought. The problems of making a fugue intelligible are not necessarily as great as they are on other keyboard instruments, but it is really hard to choose between one and the other. On stringed keyboard instruments one has the disadvantages of non-sustaining, but on the organ the advantages of sustaining are countered by all sorts of acoustical disadvantages and by lack of flexibility, not to mention the inadequacies that are delivered from the hands of the organ builder.

Another puzzling feature of Bach's handling of instrumental sound is his ability to write or transcribe the same piece for totally different instruments such as the harpsichord, organ, or violin, or to write the same unidiomatic melodic lines for an instrument and a voice. Many transcriptions of concerto movements turn up in the cantatas, sometimes even with words and choral parts superposed on them, as in the opening chorus of Cantata 146 which is based on the slow movement of the D minor Harpsichord Concerto, where the harpsichord part, probably originally a violin part, is now given to the organ as in the adaptation in its prelude of the first movement of the same concerto. (But Bach never seems to have thrown any of the pieces of the *WTC* into the emergencies of providing a new cantata for the next Sunday. In fact, it is quite striking that even some of the fugues the most totally choral in style seem never to have had words set to them.) Most of the time Bach is using the keyboard not to suggest itself, but to suggest something that lies beyond it. If one listens to four- and five-voice fugues only in terms of the sounds that the keyboard instrument is making, one hears, as Pasquali would have, a rather unsatisfactory succession of not very interesting chords.

Throughout the history of keyboard music we find deliberate evocations of other instruments: imitations of string writing (Bach himself does this in his adaptations to the keyboard of the Italian string concerto), imitations of wind instruments, of brass, trumpet calls (Prelude D II), woodwind instruments (Prelude A II), tympani (Prelude D II). From the time of William Byrd, keyboard music has always imitated the language of the contemporary instrumental or vocal ensemble. One could almost say that the relationship of key-board music to vocal and instrumental ensembles is analogous to that of graphic arts to painting. Just as graphic art is constantly sug-gesting what it is not, as it is constantly using dots to suggest lines and lines to suggest mass, so keyboard music is constantly using separate notes to suggest melodic lines, and melodic lines to suggest the interactions of harmony. Both in music and graphic art, much can only be communicated and understood in connection with an effort of the imagination, on the part of both the artist and his audi-ence. Perhaps it is this very effort of the imagination that most counts in the *WTC*.

I am reminded of a conversation with Paul Hindemith about his early transcriptions for strings of the fugues of the *WTC*. He con-fessed his disappointment with the results. One might say that every-thing was stated flatfootedly, without equivocation, and that in one sense poetry had been reduced to prose. One might easily expect a kind of fulfillment in making clear all those things which the key-board can only suggest.

More important than the actual material of any artistic medium is what the medium can suggest. A perfectly developed medium which does not suggest anything beyond or above itself is bound to fail to set in motion that vibration between executant and hearer which we call communication. No musical communication can take place if it fails to provoke musical experience.

Perhaps the very opposition with which the artist is confronted by the tools and materials of his medium is a stimulant necessary in some measure to the intensity and concentration of his communica-tion through domination of that medium. Perhaps this is why any notion of progress in the sense of technological perfection does not seem valid in terms of the time-honored tools of various artistic me-dia. Despite recent efforts, we have never entirely succeeded in mechanizing painting. Most great painting has been accomplished by relatively crude and primitive tools, which can sometimes be con-sidered as mere extensions of our own equally crude and primitive bodies.

In terms of actual organ or harpsichord registration, a great deal of what I hear in performance sounds to me capricious, irrelevant, absurd, and downright silly. But what gives me pause is a phenomenon like Anton Webern's instrumentation of the six-part Ricercar from the *Musical Offering*. This is done in his well-known pointillist style with notes in a given voice shifting from instrument to instrument. It flagrantly violates almost every generalization that I might have formulated for the art of playing fugue. There is almost no procedure in it that I would personally espouse, and yet to my ear the result is one of absolutely ravishing beauty. Whether this is because of the imposition of a totally extraneous set of dimensions and the creation of a kind of dynamic clash, I am unable to explain.

Much has been said about the desirability of returning music of the past to the instruments for which it was composed. I am not always certain whether it is because of their advantages that one may prefer them. Should this be the case, there may be a danger in allowing the medium to dominate over its intended purpose. There may be advantages in the idiomatic suitability of certain instruments to the music written for them. After all, one always prefers to read a literary work of any merit in its original language. But language itself is a medium sufficiently recalcitrant to be counted upon to extort a high degree of intensity and discipline from those who propose to master it. If I were to be asked the reasons for my choice of playing the *WTC* or any other keyboard works of Bach on the harpsichord or the clavichord, I would be obliged to reply that I have not been drawn to these instruments as much by the apparent advantages they may present as by their disadvantages. In many a piece Bach asks the keyed instruments to do the impossible. This is the challenge presented by nearly every Bach saraband and by every slow fugue. In the effort to make a saraband sing, to make a stiff instrument flexible, one is struggling with exactly the same problems that the composer himself confronted in his desire to subject these instruments to the domination of an overriding and transcendent musical idea.

One may wonder, especially in the case of the *WTC*, how much difference the choice of instrument may make, as long as we can say something with it. When I wrote my little Scarlatti catechism I felt so strongly the paramount importance of the musical idea that throughout it I never once mentioned the harpsichord or any other instrument. In the next three chapters I shall be dealing with questions that are fundamental to every kind of musical expression.

In the *WTC* there are fugues which form a fully formulated set of statements, complete and definite to the point almost of apparent rigidity. Yet it would be difficult to point out music that lends itself to being exhibited in more widely varying aspects. Its adaptability is attested not only by widely divergent interpretations but also by the widely divergent possibilities presented by different instruments. Perhaps Bach made no specific designation of instrument in the same way that the sculptor may not specify the nature of the lighting under which his work is to be seen, or even the materials in which it is to be cast. He may have created an organization of forms which is so fundamental and so expressive that it can be subjected to a variety of contexts and yet still retain its integrity and meaning. Something of the sort happens with the *WTC* when played on one instrument, or another.

I cannot say that I consider any keyboard instrument adequate to express fully on its own terms what is in this music. The clavichord reveals such qualities of nuance, of subtlety, and of immediate vocal response that in many ways I have always preferred it as a vehicle for the *WTC*, not that I think there are any grounds for asserting that the *WTC* was written specifically for it. Only in more recent years have I responded to the challenge of the harpsichord for the performance of the *WTC*. On the harpsichord strong contrasts, strong articulation, and rhythmic characterizations dominate over harmonic inflection. The harpsichord is in many ways more highly selective, much more limited. The clavichord offers a yielding, soft material, comparable to that presented to the sculptor by soft clay or wax. The harpsichord offers a hard and more resistant material like granite or marble. The differences in medium, the difference in sound, the difference in devices that have to be used to accomplish the same fundamental musical ends can be very revealing, not only to the player but also to the listener. This is why, when the time came to record the *WTC*, I insisted on playing it complete on both clavichord and harpsichord. I felt that neither instrument alone presented an adequate picture. Actually, had I been better qualified as an organist, I would have insisted on playing an organ version as well.

And why not the *WTC* on the piano? After all, it is difficult to prove that the *WTC* represents really idiomatic writing for either harpsichord or clavichord. The piano has many advantages, partic-

ularly in sustained fugues, and certain kinds of part-writing are easier to make clear on the piano. The obscurities on the modern piano
of tenor and bass, often difficult to surmount in ensemble music, can
in solo music to a certain extent be clarified by a player who has
complete control over dynamics and nuance, and who has a complete vocabulary of articulation. When first I sit down to play a fugue
on the modern piano, I am impressed by certain apparent advantages, yet later when the enchantment wears off I find the instrument
leading me toward a stylistic hybridization that has little to do with
what would have been Bach's own handling of the keyboard. I have
been led into a translation which, though it may convey some of the
meaning, has been substituted for Bach's original language. (For a
comparable hybridization verging on the preposterous, see Example
3 in chapter 6.)

   Some of those who play the *WTC* on the piano might wish to bear
in mind a set of precepts which I formulated in 1971:
1. Remember that much of Bach is not idiomatic keyboard music,
   but an imitation of voices, instruments, or ensembles, and use
   the resources of the piano accordingly.
2. Take inspiration from the possibilities of the harpsichord and
   clavichord and from what they may suggest to augment the resources of ordinary pianism, but do not attempt to imitate them
   as such.
3. On the other hand, do not allow the idiom and the possibilities of
   the piano to provoke disproportionate exaggerations and stylistic
   anachronisms.
4. Treat temptations to provocative eccentricity and to striking superficial effects with the contempt they deserve.
5. If you are determined to make Bach sound like something else,
   then *play* something else.
6. You will inevitably play Bach your way, but never cease to search
   for what might have been his, and to relate your own to it.
7. "Bach's way" is only insufficiently revealed by documents or by
   historical facts or accidents; it is more adequately revealed by the
   proportions and inner necessities of his music.
8. "Bach's way" embodies an endless variety of possibilities.
9. "Bach's way" captured, kills music; "Bach's way" followed, con-
   fers on it infinite life.

Relative Validity of Varying Opinions on the *WTC*

If I consult Spitta or Schweitzer, or any other writing about a given piece, I may find a comment which states the exact opposite of what I believe. If I inspect the work of an editor, I may see totally different indications of tempo and character from those which I think correct. On hearing someone else play a piece, I may think: "Really, how is it possible to go so far off the track?" I myself may be taken to task for something of whose validity I am totally convinced. I may listen to certain "Bach specialists" and come to the conclusion that of all possible ways of doing things they have chosen the wrongest. How is one going to sort this out? When is one right, when is one wrong? Is it possible to find criteria by which we can check and counter-check an opinion? It helps, I think, to know something about the nature and circumstances of the original performance and about the possibilities inherent in the instruments that Bach was using. When someone took me to task for playing the C-sharp major Prelude of Book II too fast, my answer could have been: "Well, just try to make that sound on either the harpsichord or the clavichord at the tempo you suggest!" Yet this prelude could have been brought to sound absolutely marvelous on an instrument that would sustain enough to permit a slow tempo, even though in the literal sense it would have been contrary to what is likely to have been Bach's own treatment of it.

Many mistaken opinions are produced by the influences of pre-conception and habit. It is all too easy, when one has become accustomed to something, to come to the conclusion that it is right. It is also easy to be misled by the instrument on which one is playing. Unless one constantly has in mind the kind of sound with which Bach was working the piano can be very misleading. But certainly it is possible to go equally wrong when using the harpsichord or the clavichord. Generalizations derived from the common features shared by certain types of pieces, certain types of dance movements, and certain types of time signatures can be misleading. One may decide that a piece is like another piece when in fact it really is not; one may then attempt to force it into a straitjacket for which it was never intended.

I have always been suspicious of many of the theories concerning fixed relationship of pulse (or *tactus*) as applied to the music of Bach's time. If one forces through a mathematical relationship between different sections of a piece, despite the possible advantage of a certain kind of super-unity and super-organization, there is the danger of creating an undesirable monotony. Most of the best chamber music players with whom I have worked seem deliberately to avoid such mathematical correspondences of tempo between one movement and another. I think I know why. I once witnessed a performance of a Goldoni play in Rome that had been directed by a producer who obviously had some sort of theory about timing and tempo of speech. The result was such that I could tap the same pulse all the way through the entire play. Because everyone in this deadly performance was moving at a common rate of speed, there was no differentiation between one character and another. We all have different pulse rates; we all have different chemistry. If one wishes to give to a piece of music a characterization that is different from that of another, to endow it with a personality of its own, one may need to avoid, rather than cultivate, common relationships of tempo.

Among the many mistaken views that nevertheless achieve a considerable amount of success, there exists the possibility of a kind of genuinely creative misunderstanding. But the quality of misunderstanding depends a great deal on the qualities of the person who is doing the misunderstanding. Perhaps it is not so important *whether* one is right or wrong as *how* one is right or wrong. I personally think that Busoni's conception of the B minor Fugue in Book I embodies some serious mistakes, but Busoni's mistakes are not the mistakes of anyone of lesser stature.

Everyone has a tendency unconsciously to cast in his own image a work of art or his idea of a great artist, or for that matter to view a period of history in terms of his own time. It is not so much a question of understanding Bach wrongly or rightly as a question of capacities of consciousness and feeling. It is a question of abstaining from taking a position which in any way precludes further revelation. The mind made up need not necessarily become the equivalent of the mind closed.

CHAPTER III.

The Melodic Approach

PRELUDE: EULOGY OF THE HUMAN VOICE · A NOTE ON MELODIC
FORM · INTERVALS AND THE VOICE · MUSICAL INTERVALS WITHIN
THE CONTEXT OF A MELODY · COMPLEX ORGANIZATION OF INTER-
VALS · ESSENTIAL MELODY AND VARIOUS LEVELS OF ELABORATION ·
INFLUENCE OF VOCAL FEELING ON MELODIC ARTICULATION · ASSO-
CIATIVE ASPECTS OF MELODY · MELODY AT THE KEYBOARD · THE
CONCEPTS OF ARTICULATION, PHRASING, AND INFLECTION · EXIST-
ING AND SUGGESTED WAYS OF INDICATING ARTICULATION AND
PHRASING · THE MELODIC APPROACH TO A NEW PIECE · ULTIMATE
INSEPARABILITY OF MELODY FROM OTHER MUSICAL ELEMENTS

Prelude: Eulogy of the Human Voice

Any discussion of musical melody can most suitably begin with a
eulogy of the human voice. However, we are not so much concerned
with that kind of voice that emits ravishing sounds as with something
much more modest, the kind of voice that most of us have. Most of
us are equipped to whistle, hum, grunt, squeak, or scratch at some
sort of pitch. (If there was ever a piece of good advice, it was Tovey's remark at the beginning of his edition of the *WTC*: "If there is
anything you don't understand in a piece of music, undertake to sing
it.")[1] In my sense, the ability to sing means primarily the ability to
sing as for one's self, the ability to sharpen one's ear. The noises
emitted may not be very pleasing to anyone else, but what is neces-

1. Bach, J. S.: *Forty-Eight Preludes and Fugues* . . . Edited by Donald Francis
Tovey . . . London, The Associated Board of the R.A.M. & the R.C.M. [1924].

sary is somehow to land on the accurate pitch at the right time. If this can be done, the evidence is fairly good that one has thoroughly heard what is involved, and that one has made an important beginning toward a conception of how it works. If there is any shortcut to achieving a feeling for every aspect of harmony and tonality, as well as for melody, it is the ability to sing every note of a piece in such fashion that when one hears a modulation, one knows where one is in relation to the tonic, that in a piece in C, for example, one is capable of sensing the drama of the difference between C major and E major. One has only to think of the "first" and "second" themes of Beethoven's *Waldstein* Sonata. This points to the sort of awareness that the habit of singing everything can give.

Not only does the vocal approach, the ability to sing every note, furnish an inside track into the very essence of any music with which one is dealing, but it provides a tremendous aid to the musical memory. In dealing with pupils, I have many times discovered that those passages which were not securely lodged in the student's memory were those which had not been clearly heard. For myself, I know that passages that in any way escape me usually turn out to be either those in which my hearing has not been sufficiently sharpened, or those in which it has been dulled by the sound of the instrument or by the acoustics of the hall. If anything on an off night can bring one back when one has had lapses of concentration, it is that blind animal homing sense that dogs have, and birds, and people who sing the notes of pieces they play.

A Note on Melodic Form

Melody in the abstract, that is, on paper, is organized in very much the same way as any aggregation of elements that produces a recognizable shape or set of shapes in any medium. Anyone who has taken an elementary art course or who has read a treatise on design has undoubtedly dealt with the placing of objects—with making groups of one, two, and three, forming other groups and then forming larger groups out of the initial groups; and with setting up relationships of singularity, plurality, identity, and dissimilarity. These same relationships exist in the organization of musical tones. The grammar of melodic form is almost universally applicable. When for the first time I read a collection of Paul Klee's writings and lectures, *Das bildnerische Denken* (Basel, 1956), I discovered a method of exposition and a terminology with which as a musician I found myself in complete sympathy.

It is significant however that the only two dimensions of music which lend themselves to translation into visual terms are those of melody and rhythm. Any attempt to find a visual counterpart for harmony leads to insurmountable problems. But melody and rhythm obey in simple enough fashion the universal laws of form and of human perception of it. And certainly these common elements appear as well in the materials of language and grammar.

But melody and melodic form remain in the domain of the abstract unless they are given a physically experienceable meaning. What brings melody to life is its evocation of the human voice, whether in real or in imaginary singing. Each interval, each contour of a melody that is sung has its own specific feel and becomes more than mere information; it becomes part of the material of experience. We become participants in a beautiful form, lifted out of what we may regard as our habitual ugliness and disorder.

Intervals and the Voice

Even if one thinks one knows in advance what an interval will sound and feel like, it should be reexamined in its own context. One can take a fresh look at the old familiar seconds, major and minor, the same old thirds, fourths, fifths, sixths, and sevenths, and even the octave or the twelfth can reveal surprises when considered melodically. So can larger intervals, even those that we cannot sing, those that we can only imagine, like twentieths. Not only each interval but also the recurrence of an interval can have an individuality all its own. All too easily it is possible to hear intervals only in terms of habit or in relation to the prevailing acoustics. In eliminating ready-made generalizations, as we take the vocal approach to intervals, we have the opportunity of finding out what we really feel about them, even if we never discover precisely why we feel as we do. In the light of a fresh approach thus taken, it becomes possible to ask ourselves if we really feel about a given passage as we may have thought or said we did, or whether our instrumental treatment of the passage really corresponds to our vocal feeling about it.

Furthermore, one can discover a surprising amount of agreement among entirely different individuals about the results of such experiments. When I have persuaded pupils to sing a given passage freely and easily, I have discovered that they will arrive independently at exactly the same results. We are dealing with a level of hearing which is so fundamental that, once achieved, it predominates over the divergences that might be possible on the surface.

In practicing this exercise with intervals, it is advisable to make no prescription whatsoever for the kind of syllables that are to be pronounced. But a preliminary examination might be recommended using vowels only, because with vowels it immediately becomes clear which intervals are convenient and which are not. There obviously exists some natural tendency toward the introduction of consonants that will facilitate hitting the note on pitch. If one were to sing the subject of the B-flat minor Fugue of Book I (Example 3.1), or for that matter almost any other fugue subject of the *WTC*, on an uninterrupted vowel sound, the result would be quite unsatisfactory. In fact it would be very difficult to keep from sounding aspirates in order to make the intonation more precise. This of course is quite natural. Some intervals will seem to demand the introduction of some kind of consonant. This is the sort of thing that happens in differentiating between conjunct and disjunct motion. For something completely absurd, one might try singing the C minor Fugue of Book I (Example 3.2) on an uninterrupted vowel sound. One may further consider the differences between conjunct and disjunct motions in the Fugues in D major and D-sharp minor of Book II.

Example 3.1 Fugue B-flat minor, I

There is no greater fallacy than measuring vocal intervals by the piano. One of the principal factors contributing to the insecurity and unmusicality of singers is their habit of taking from the piano the

Example 3.2   Fugue C minor, I

note that they are seeking. If the piano is in tune, it condemns them to a tempered intonation which in any case is unnatural to a singer. Rather, if a D is wanted in the key of B-flat, it should be taken not from D, but from B-flat. It is the measurement of an interval that creates its significance, not its component notes. Often one is struck by the musicality of certain totally untrained singers. Their voices may not stand up to the exigencies of public performance, but very often they have all or a great many of the natural musical instincts. The trained singer has come up against very much the same set of problems as the trained instrumentalist. The necessity to whittle and file, remold and refine the medium in which he is working has often taken all freshness and spontaneity out of it. The exercises that one has had to practice in order to play evenly and steadily on the piano and the vocalises that one has gone through in order to get the voice under absolute control are most of them unmusical if not antimusical. Once one has mastered one's craft or one's voice, the problem remains of rediscovering music, the very purpose for which presumably one went through all this effort!

Musical Intervals within the Context of a Melody

Stepwise progressions lend themselves to vowel sounds and certainly are the most comfortable to sing. They are an age-old method of binding together the notes of a composition. But a change of melodic direction is an eventful occurrence for the voice whether or not it embodies a temporary diatonic decoration or makes a salient point in the melodic outline. It should be noted whether large or small leaps are involved and whether the changes of melodic direction incorporate themselves easily into curves. The contours of the D-sharp minor Fugue of Book I are not as angular as those of the B-flat minor Fugue of Book I, but those of the A minor Fugue of Book II are really jagged. No one is likely to sing its subject on a single vowel. Those notes that stick out of the prevailing melodic direction are sometimes important parts of the melodic contour, but generally they are either suggestions of another voice or merely subsidiary decorations, as in the E-flat major Fugue of Book II (Example 3.3). Compare, for example, the harmonic skeleton of the opening of the A minor Prelude of Book II with its written text (Example 3.4).

If the keyboard is not infused with some sort of vocal sense, it is scarcely more eloquent than a typewriter. The vocal sense, and its capacity in reality or in imagination to participate in musical intervals, is not only important to the hearing of a single line, but is also probably the most important factor in the hearing of polyphony. One hears counterpoint far less in terms of its component notes than in terms of the transitions between these notes. If on a keyboard instrument one hears what sounds like a series of rather unsatisfactory non-sustaining chords instead of hearing a fugue, this is because one is not being made to hear the melodic relationships of notes.

Of course all sorts of influences can be brought to bear on melodic material, and up to now we have not attempted to isolate them. In experimenting with musical intervals, one is bound to find that some intervals have a greater similarity among themselves than others, and

Example 3.3   Fugue E-flat major, II

Example 3.4 Prelude A minor, II

that anything which is recognizable as part of a chord seems to be easier to sing. One knows already where one is going. The influence of tonal or enharmonic function can be very great. We hear Example 3.5 in terms of C minor, but in its enharmonic notation in the context of Example 3.6, we recognize the opening of the C-sharp minor Fugue in Book I. But on the keyboard we have heard exactly the same intervals. Rhythmic configurations can exert considerable influence on the feel of intervals. One must be prepared for the infinite

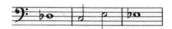

Example 3.5 Fugue C-sharp minor, I, in enharmonic notation

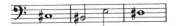

Example 3.6 Fugue C-sharp minor, I

variability of even the most familiar. Until an interval is tried out,
one will never know its true significance.

Complex Organization of Intervals

It is hard to find a melody in the *WTC* that does not contain the
elements of more than one voice. In fact, in all but a handful of
fugue subjects, the outlining of harmony is immediately apparent.
In many of the preludes, the ostensible two-part writing merely serves
to indicate a much fuller harmony. In the D-sharp minor Prelude of
Book II, one has the choice of hearing the upper part at its opening
as actually written in one voice, or as a decoration in two voices of
an ascending diatonic scale (Example 3.7). The choice may depend
on how much one may want to savor all the melodic details. I like
to play it in such a way as to obtain both the harmonic generalities
and the melodic particulars. Sometimes in the initial statement of a
fugue subject its later harmonic implications may be only partially
prefigured, to be realized fully only after the entrance of other voices.
The pathetic intervals and expressive leaps inherent in the subject of
the D-sharp minor Fugue of Book II might perhaps be considered to
foreshadow the combinations of basic materials that ultimately achieve
an almost excruciating level of intensity. The beginning of the B
major Fugue of Book II (Example 3.8) might be heard as an arpeggiation of a chord of the sixth on B (Example 3.9). But such a banal

Example 3.7 Prelude D-sharp minor, II

interpretation is completely belied by Bach's later harmonizations of the subject.

Essential Melody and Various Levels of Elaboration

A simple irreducible vocal melody underlies most melodic construction, no matter what degree of decoration may have been imposed upon it. (This reminds one of the simple geometric forms elaborated by the great Baroque architects.) But irreducible vocal melodies are relatively rare in Bach. For the most part, Bach's melodies already embody some degree of elaboration. The verbal counterpart of the irreducible melody, even though absurd, might be a simple sentence: Man bites dog. One can then elaborate. Dark-haired man bites brown dog. Dark-haired man slowly prepares to bite brown dachshund dog. And so forth. The possibilities of elaboration by means of qualifying words and dependent clauses are virtually without limit. In a comparable manner Bach builds up his melodic layers by the introduction of changing notes, passing notes, and figurations that elaborate simpler contours. In fugues like the D minor and C-sharp minor of Book II, one can strip off all the decorations to versions respectively

Example 3.8 Fugue B major, II

Example 3.9 Fugue B major, II, harmonic outline

in eighth notes and dotted eighth notes that throughout make perfect sense. In Bach, something of the relationship of the old vocal melody to instrumental diminution remains visible in the notation. For his fugues in vocal style, he generally uses large notes like those in the C-sharp minor Fugue of Book I or in the B-flat minor Fugue of Book I, and the decorations in such fugues partaking of the *stile antico* are seldom noted in anything smaller than quarters and occasional eighth notes. This is the kind of notation that is familiar in texts of sixteenth- and seventeenth-century vocal music that have not been subjected by editors to the debatable reduction of note values. (For this reason, I am bitterly opposed to the practice of reducing note values in editing sixteenth-century keyboard music. What in the note picture is immediately recognizable as vocal, and therefore as an essential part of the melody as distinguishable from diminution and instrumental decoration, becomes far less intelligible once the note values have been reduced.)

When there is free arpeggiation and not altogether strict part-writing, all sorts of ambiguities may present themselves to anyone attempting to sort out the various melodic levels. In the F minor Prelude of Book I, for instance, it is not desirable to hear all the sixteenth notes in terms of a consistent two- or even three-part melodic texture, but rather in terms of the ambiguities of part-writing with which we are so familiar in allemandes or in other dance pieces which represent decorations of an unstated simpler version. In such pieces it can be very helpful to sing the equivalent of one voice of a continuo part. If this continuo part is reduced to a minimum of activity, with as many common tones and as much diatonic motion as possible, it forms a kind of guide through the complexities of the piece.

Influence of Vocal Feeling on Melodic Articulation

The influence of our vocal feeling upon melodic articulation is evident in the devices that we use to negotiate different intervals, whether we stick to vowels, whether we aspirate them for greater security, or whether we resort to consonants. And if indeed we resort to consonants, we have an infinite variety of them at our disposal. We have the hard percussive consonants and the labial sounds. It is very difficult for example to connect k, k, k; but la, la, la, la can be connected quite nicely. Every conceivable degree of articulation has its

counterpart in speech, a fact that exposes the absurdity of systema-
tized articulation, the absurdity of deciding in advance that certain
note values are to be shortened to a half or to a quarter. (In this
sense, one can take the measure of a performance of the Beethoven
G major Concerto from its opening piano phrase. Either it will speak
or it will not.) If a fine, icy, abstract effect is desired, this systemi-
zation will enhance it splendidly, but it will have no relationship
whatever to the expressive qualities of speech, or even to the expressive capacities of musical intervals. This is why I do not take an
altogether approving view of French solfège, which reduces all intervals to a detaché, to a sounding of monosyllabic names of notes.
It is exceedingly efficient in cultivating a sense of accuracy and ex-
actitude in musical perception, but it does not necessarily refine the
nuances of musical feeling. It identifies notes and helps to produce
them immediately and accurately, but it does not show the relationships among those notes.

Although hitherto we have been speaking about what appears to
be fundamentally natural musical declamation, it is perfectly clear
that, ever since words were first set to music, their pronunciation in
conjunction with music has added a different dimension. While the
presence of words may not alter fundamental musical relationships,
it superposes certain qualifications. The relationship between the
rhythm of speech and that of music is a very mysterious one, and
that is part of its fascination. When words and music achieve a satisfactory collaboration, miracles occur like those in the songs of
Schubert and Dowland and, despite his later indifference to prosody,
in certain of Bach's ariosos and early cantatas.

Associative Aspects of Melody

In melody associated with rhythm one discovers all sorts of suggestions of locomotion as well as of effort expended in overcoming the
force of gravity; there are suggested ascents and descents, leaps and
falls. The relative degree of distance represented in the span of intervals gives rise to a sense of space, as it does, for instance, in the
B-flat minor Fugue of Book I. Surely most of us associate the minor
ninth F to G-flat with a sense of span (see Example 3.1). I have
found most enlightening the experience not only of walking a melody, but also of taking steps that correspond to the relative width and

direction of its intervals. Each time that I have asked a pupil to do this he has returned to the keyboard instrument as if infused with a sense of new life. What before may not have made sense now begins to do so simply because something has happened that has provoked an experience. And part of an experience is the physical perception of the difference, and the degree of difference, between one thing and another.

A similar and very revealing activity is the performance of a melodic line with one finger. Not only does it produce a keen sense of the negotiation of space, but it also operates on a level comparable to the functioning of the voice. In playing with one finger the subject of the C minor Fugue of Book I, one discovers the necessity of measuring all the intervals quite carefully (see Example 3.2). In measuring them that carefully, one experiences them even more intensely. (My friend Arthur Loesser used to produce a ravishing performance of the Chopin E-flat Nocturne while using a pencil for the right-hand part.) One could learn a great deal about two-part inventions, or for that matter about any two-voice pieces, by playing each voice with one finger. The revelations yielded even by such a relatively simple piece as the A minor Prelude of Book I (see Example 6.1) can be quite astonishing.

Some of the foregoing may be related to the historical development of keyboard playing, in the sense that the earliest methods of fingering all operated two by two, like stepping. Beyond the voice's approach to one note at a time, there exists in the history of keyboard music a progression toward multiple simultaneous approaches, from the ringing of bells with a single hand depressing one lever at a time, which in its way is like hopping, to the present-day two-fist handling of the carillon keyboard, which is like stepping. Out of this development came early keyboard fingering, which also proceeds in units of two, like stepping, except for the use of several pairs of fingers. For all its efficiency, our full ten-finger system has a tendency to divorce us from the real feeling of what we are playing. We have never really learned to move in units of ten. The decimal system is a rationalistic institution, more useful for calculation than for meaningful bodily movement. Our physical organism conducts itself primarily in ones and twos. A distance hopped on one foot feels quite different from that same distance stepped. Stepping is easier, and the experience less intense, and so on, down to the totally adulterated remnant of experience that is to be derived from the unimaginatively employed ten-finger system.

Melody at the Keyboard

Keyboard instruments lack many of the more natural qualities of other instruments, especially wind instruments, which benefit by their close alliance with the necessities of breathing. I have always felt that players of single-line instruments showed a far greater melodic sensibility than most players of keyboard instruments. There is a very sinister, button-pushing aspect to keyboard instruments; they constantly threaten to level and destroy many of the melodic beauties that the composer has written into his music. The role of the interpreter, after all, is to enrich, not to impoverish. The keyboard player is led into this impoverishment not only by the nature of his instrument but also by the insufficiencies of his own ear. There is a constant danger of hearing merely keyboard sound rather than compelling the keyboard to communicate a translation of the real vocal essence of the music. Seldom does anyone play as well as he sings. By this I mean singing in the musical sense, not in the sense of a professional singer, who all too frequently is profoundly unmusical, or has been rendered so by his teachers.

It often happens that the more one becomes distracted by the sound of a keyboard instrument or by its technical difficulties, the more vocal inflection is allowed to go by the board. Often one can hear the initial entry of a fugue subject beautifully played, beautifully phrased, but when the following entries appear against other voices they fail to hold their own. One must constantly ask whether two voices are being played together as well as they were played separately. I always make every pupil of mine play and sing not only every voice separately but also every voice against the remaining voices. This helps. But again and again, after the voices have been put together they no longer sound as they did when they were alone; the ability to hear them has diminished and the ability to project them has slackened. This can happen even after everything has supposedly been sorted out; or the piece may have been played so much that it needs sorting out again. A four-part or five-part fugue risks being heard merely in terms of the sound that comes from the instrument. If this happens, there is nothing to do but to go into the workshop with it, take it all apart again, and rehear it, line by line, note by note.

I sometimes wonder whether any keyboard concept has done more damage to musical sense than the notion of the singing tone on the piano. Heaven knows I can say this, coming from the rattling, squeaking, recalcitrant instrument that I am obliged to make sound as if it were making music, even though I cannot entertain even the illusion of doing anything about a "singing tone" in the abstract. If a harpsichord or any other instrument has been made to "sing," it is because the notes have been put into a context that makes them sound as if they really were being sung. What passes for a singing tone is the relationship of that tone with other tones and the rightness and meaningfulness of its context. With considerable bitterness, I think of time wasted in my youth being concerned about a singing tone, when I would have done better to examine questions of articulation and phrasing. It is not the notes themselves but the intervals between them that constitute a melody. One may say that the greatest playing is done as much between as on the notes. (One means of course between and not beside the notes!) In other words, great playing plays the right notes but it also plays what connects those notes, what gives those notes meaning.

The difference is quite striking between a Bach melody and a melody of the nineteenth century or even an Italianate cantilena of one of Bach's contemporaries such as Handel. Probably the reason for this difference is to be found in the essentially crystalline structure of the Bach melody. The elements that compose it, as well as the details that elaborate it, retain their identity. They do not flow imperceptibly into one another like certain forms of liquids and semiliquids. The Bach melody is composed of large crystals with accretions of smaller crystals, which remain distinguishable, even when overlapping or interfused.

The Concepts of Articulation, Phrasing, and Inflection

In the preface to the first volume of my edition of sixty Scarlatti sonatas, to the question, "What is phrasing?" I answer: "Phrasing is the uniting and organizing in performance of what belongs together, and the separation of what belongs apart. Furthermore it is the demonstration of the relationships of notes; it is the demonstration of the differences and gradations of activity and passivity, of tension and relaxation. It parallels the organization, balancing, and punctuation of gesture and of speech."

To the question, "What is articulation?" I answer: "Articulation, in the sense in which I use the word, is a subsidiary of phrasing. Articulation is the mere detaching or connecting of notes."

To these definitions I might add the concept of melodic inflection, which is the placing of various degrees of intensity and accentuation. On some instruments this is accomplished by devices of articulation, on others by means of dynamics. Much inflection through dynamics is affected by harmonic and rhythmic functions and is difficult to relate uniquely to the melodic aspects of music. Furthermore I know of no such consistency of the vocal sense in matters of dynamics as is observable in matters of articulation.

The notion of associating dynamics with pitch is dubious in any classical style. Small-town piano teachers have told many of us: "Whenever a melody goes up, make a crescendo, and when it comes down, make a diminuendo." Obviously this is utterly childish, and really disastrous when applied to Bach. There are other factors, mainly harmonic, that affect dynamics far more than melodic contour. Given the granular structure and relatively jagged outline of Bach's melodies, not to mention the nature of his harmony, the application of swellbox crescendo and diminuendo dynamics does not work. It takes away more than it gives.

Existing and Suggested Ways of Indicating Articulation and Phrasing

The crude and primitive system that we have used since the nineteenth century in our musical notation for indicating phrasing, articulation, and dynamics is trying, as it were, with one hand to do the work of several dozen hands. Like the conductor's beat it is trying to suggest things in the most general and often necessarily vague way. How many different musical elements must a conductor be able to suggest to his orchestra, and with what primitive means does he do it? The drawback of both of these systems is that they are totally non-analytic, and if something goes wrong it goes terribly wrong without much likelihood of rectifying itself. On the other hand, when the system works well, everything is miraculously and mysteriously welded into a kind of unity that the analytical approach to isolated elements can never conceivably achieve. So we are caught eternally and inextricably in the confusion between the general and the particular, and no matter how sophisticated we may be about either one, the result is always going to be slightly a matter of chance and of rather primitive guesswork.

In my Scarlatti preface I suggest methods of indicating articulation and phrasing that principally can be reduced to this: "For breaks, ꞌ or V; for indivisible connections, square brackets, ⌐⌐; for partially connected divisions, broken square brackets, ⌐⌐; for small divisions embraced by a larger division, concentric square brackets, ⌐⌐⌐ ; for detachment, dots, • ; for emphasis, tenuto marks, __. Large phrases can be marked / at the beginnings and \ at the ends, without obscuring the note picture with extended square brackets. Slurs ⌒ should only be used for what is actually to be played legato, for what vocally would embrace but a single syllable. Slurs embracing several syllables or several divisions of articulation are misleading."

Musical phrasing is the exposition of shape. Just as good speech makes absolutely clear what is being said, good phrasing in music must show what is alike and what is different, and further heighten the sense of form by making clear the relationship of the parts to the whole while rendering it all completely intelligible, convincing, and moving. It achieves eloquence in detail while it bridges the span of the whole, and it liberates all the vital forces inherent in the piece.

In dealing with Bach we have a very great need to bypass the editors. It is essential to settle questions of articulation for oneself, even though the same conclusions as those of the editor may emerge. Once written down, most editorial indications for articulation are ambiguous or downright misleading. With the aid of the player's vocal sense, articulations are far better arrived at independently. After all, keyboard players have every reason to profit by their relative freedom. Unlike string players they are not obliged to sit in orchestras playing other people's bowings. They have a perfectly autonomous existence and might just as well profit by it.

The Melodic Approach to a New Piece

The first essential step in a melodic approach to a new piece is to sing everything, in order to get the feel of its component intervals and their relationships, and to discover the hierarchy of what is essentially melodic and what in a subsidiary way is decorative. But some further questions can be asked. They concern the identification of the largest musical divisions of the piece, the next largest, and so on, and, starting from the other end, the smallest units, the next smallest, and so on. (These last two procedures became known in my studio respectively as taking the bird's-eye or the worm's-eye point of view!) They also concern the identification of those notes that form themselves into indivisible groups as well as the breaks between groups. The remaining questions direct themselves toward the discovery of higher organizations of phrase structure. One asks of a group of notes whether it comes to a full stop before the beginning of the next group or whether the end of one group also forms the beginning of what follows. Further questions also ask which among several breaks between groups of notes are primary and which are secondary. Which correspond to periods, which to commas, which to breaks between words or between syllables?

Ultimate Inseparability of Melody from Other Musical Elements

And then comes the synthesis. After absorbing all the questioning and analysis into one's instinctive feeling about the piece, one must adjust the articulation and phrasing to the particular qualities and capacities of the instrument. This will confirm the ultimate inseparability of melody from other musical elements and the relativity of all articulation, depending not only on the instrument that is being played, but on the acoustical conditions and a host of other contributory factors.

None of this excludes the possibility of introducing arbitrary modifications into the natural articulation, either for the sake of a further musical end or as a result of other modifications, for instance the new dimension that words add. But all of these complexities are more likely to resolve themselves if one has exposed oneself thoroughly to the expressive capacities of the basic inherent melodic relationships by singing.

CHAPTER IV.
The Rhythmic Approach

OUR PHYSICAL RELATIONSHIP TO RHYTHM · SOME CHARACTERISTICS
OF METER · THE PROBLEM OF A DISTINCTION BETWEEN METER AND
RHYTHM · SOME ELEMENTS OF RHYTHM · THE FORMATION OF
RHYTHMIC GROUPINGS, OR RHYTHMIC SYLLABLES · RHYTHMIC PO-
LYPHONY · RHYTHM AND IMAGINARY MOVEMENT · SUMMARY OF ES-
SENTIAL RHYTHMIC RELATIONSHIPS AND MEANS OF EXPRESSION

Our Physical Relationship to Rhythm

Our most direct physical relationship to rhythm probably comes from
our pulse and from our sense of the passage of time as measured by
that pulse and with it our sense of meter. The rhythm of breathing
and the habit of speech are also of great importance in our physical
comprehension of rhythm. But perhaps most important of all, certainly in the style of music that we are here discussing, is the asso-
ciation of rhythm with movement, with locomotion in time, with
displacement of the body, with counteracting of the force of gravity,
and with the kind of energy that needs to be expended in order to
perform any given movement or gesture in a particular length of
time. Much of what I will presently have to say concerns the various
degrees of activity, effort, and repose in performing any imaginary
locomotion or counteracting the force of gravity.

Some Characteristics of Meter

The simplest way of beginning a discussion of meter, I suppose, is
to refer to a series of undifferentiated beats, to the inhuman ticking

of a watch or a metronome. We all know that it is impossible for us to observe anything and retain it without organizing it into some sort of form. In order not only to recognize an identity between one group and another, in that they are composed of similar patterns, but also to group the groups in their turn, we must attribute to them a dissimilarity. Thus measures two, three, and four of a four-bar phrase cannot sound like measure one. Otherwise there would be only four one-bar phrases.

In a duple meter we consider two as an upbeat to one. Two is the going somewhere; one is the arriving, if you like. So we perceive a distinction between upbeats and downbeats. The basic function of an upbeat is to produce the event that results in the downbeat. It is much more telling to feel how you get there than to learn afterwards how you got there. The downbeat is history and the upbeat experience. A term that I very often use in contrast to upbeat is afterbeat, which describes a feminine ending, or a trailing off. An afterbeat constitutes a follow-through of a happening that has already taken place, as in the G minor Fugue of Book II (Example 4.1).

Example 4.1 Fugue G minor, II

In a triple measure there are two ways of handling the offbeats. There is the way practiced by the French in the eighteenth century, that is, regarding the triple measure as an unequal measure in two. In other words, it is counted one, three, one, three, one, beaten with a downbeat on one and an upbeat on three, and there is also the possibility of regarding it as ♩♩♩|♩♩♩|. One can push the measure ahead with a second beat, but one has a little more leeway with the third beat, where there is a natural spacing resembling the unequal measure of the French: ♩♩|♩. Nevertheless the role of the two can be quite varied. To make a four-beat measure distinguishable in performance from a duple measure, the role of the second and third beats has to be different from what it would be if they were merely second and first beats in a duple measure.

Many are the measures in which the real upbeat begins immediately after the downbeat, or even with the first subdivision after the downbeat. There may be complex upbeats, the characterization and function of which can differ as widely as the possible ways of leaping from the ground and returning to it. These characteristics carry themselves in Western music into the compound measures and have a tendency, which twentieth-century composers boldly fight, to dominate even rhythms of 5s and 7s, and other prime numbers. There is a strong tendency on everybody's part to divide them into 2s and 3s. For a performer, the methods of differentiating one part of a measure from another are very subtle; at times they seem merely telepathic. They usually involve accents, however faint, that may be dynamic or agogic, that is, produced by a very slight lengthening of the stressed tone.

By and large, those parts of the measure which are active and which control the establishment and maintenance of a tempo are the upbeats and offbeats. There is very little that can be done with a downbeat. The downbeat is a result, not a cause. But there is a great deal that can be done to manipulate the causes represented in the rest of the measure. And since two is an incipient upbeat to three, it shares with four a certain upbeat strength if a four-beat measure is in any way subdivided. For the moment, I shall not discuss the peculiarities of sextuples and further multiples.

Ways of differentiating various parts of the measure are largely determined by the fundamental harmonic movement of the piece. Very often one can tell more about the basic rhythm of a piece by looking at the progression of harmony than by looking at the time signature. Furthermore, time signatures do not necessarily indicate the character of an entire piece.

Those performers experienced in Bach, Mozart, and Beethoven and in later nineteenth-century music have an instinctive feeling for the differences between tones that are part of the main harmony and passing tones. By definition, passing tones usually occur on offbeat parts of the measure or on subdivisions of the beat. This relationship of main harmonic movements to elaborations is allied with the relationship of essential melodic movement to decoration. The hierarchies are comparable and in this style they very often work together. Ensemble players experienced in classical music give each other cues by virtue of this harmonic function, by the way in which the music itself is disposed around and within the measure. This makes it possible for them constantly to adjust to each other.

The notion that the downbeat is accented has done enormous damage. One can hear it daily. I prefer to lay emphasis on the preparation of downbeats than on their accentuation. Preparation can be so convincing that a hearer may not notice whether or not that which was prepared has been omitted. One may omit from a phrase what appears to be its most important note—if the manner of approach has been such as to make it seem inevitable, it will often give the illusion of having been heard. This phenomenon is related to the problem of playing sustained music on a non-sustaining instrument. If the preparation has been properly made—that parabola that one describes in launching an idea—the sounds of individual tones do not necessarily have to sustain themselves for their full notated value. The idea is launched in such a way that it makes a bridge across what otherwise might have been disruptive silence. It is not sound but mental expectation that produces musical continuity.

The inner portions of measures and the subdivisions of beats are always their most active parts. It is in these that every experienced ensemble player makes contact with other players and responds to them. These rather than the downbeats are the things of which the skillful conductor makes use in establishing characterizations, instead of mechanically plowing forward like a metronome. These subdivisions of measures and beats make it possible constantly to regenerate a tempo, to recapture it if it has slipped in one direction or another, or to keep it going if someone else is working against it.

It is only on the active parts of a measure or on salient, strong intervals that a convincing rubato can be based. Melodically, it is very hard to base a rubato on a stepwise progression that is unqualified by some other musical element. A rubato cannot be based on a bland consonance, but only on the activity of a dissonance that is preparing a consonance. The best and most convincing rubatos obviously are based on a sensibility to all these elements, and a balance of them.

I must confess here my inadequacy at dealing with the concept of accent. It is useless to conceal the fact that in reading theoretical treatises I often fail to understand what is meant by accent. I use the term myself, but it has a meaning for me only in the sense of an emphatic inflection. I even mistrust the word *stress*. I am more likely to talk about upbeats, downbeats, afterbeats, and active and passive portions of a measure or of a rhythmic figure.

The Problem of a Distinction between Meter and Rhythm

I should also confess that I am incapable of making a fully adequate distinction between meter and rhythm. The one that I made in my Scarlatti preface of 1953 has drawn upon itself a certain amount of justifiable criticism. I said something about meter being regular, which of course is perfectly true, and rhythm being the imposition of irregularity upon the regularity of meter. Now it is true that irregularity is an attribute of rhythm, but it is certainly no definition of it. I am not sure that I wish to undertake, now or at any point in my life, a definition of rhythm. Part of the difficulty in distinguishing these two elements derives from the fact that they often work so closely together that one is likely to be talking about one when one really means the other. What I am willing to say here is that meter, in terms of its name, can be used to measure and to control the exact dimensions of rhythmic shapes. We all know that if we stretch the meter beyond a certain point, if we play out of time, our rhythm becomes incomprehensible; we no longer have even a rhythmic shape in our phrase or in our piece. If we have broken too many of the rules that make predictability possible, we lose the attention of the hearer. If, however, a new idea is to be assimilated, it must somehow be led up to. Meter helps lead us from one thing to another so that we can relate them. If we do not have this relationship, we are in chaos, and our musical shapes all fall apart.

Fertile and provocative distinctions can be made between the rhythmical basis of prosody and the rhythms of dance, but I refrain from pursuing them here. By and large, in the style with which we are concerned, I think that dance rhythm predominates over speech rhythm, certainly in the fugues, and in most of the preludes.

Some Elements of Rhythm

One of the most important aspects of rhythm is variation of rate of speed as indicated by notes of different value, and the expressive connotations of these differentiations. I can constantly be heard speaking of these differentiations in terms of activity and repose. This is on the associative assumption that faster notes are likely to represent a greater degree of activity than slower notes or, quite obviously, rests. There are however many ways in which the activity of fast notes can be reduced and that of slow notes increased beyond their notated rhythmical character. I shall later speak of them.

Those points in almost any piece which concern the performer, and which should be investigated by him, are the moments of change of note value. A regular series of even notes, except as qualified by melody and harmony, is unlikely to be particularly eventful. But when one changes from fast notes to slow, something has happened. Were one to walk or hop across the room, the change would be felt even more intensely. One is displacing a bodily mass subject to the force of gravity. It takes more effort to perform this displacement quickly than to perform it slowly. If anyone wants fully to experience the difference between fast and slow movement, let him try hopping a few rhythmic patterns.

Much more eventful than the changes from fast to slow are the changes from slow to fast, such as quarter notes breaking into eighths and then into sixteenths. Even when merely tapping with a pencil, one discovers that an increase of effort is necessary to negotiate the faster notes. The contrast would be even greater if one were running or hopping. But whether tapping, running, or hopping, one needs to be prepared in advance for the increase in speed. Without adequate preparation, minor or even major disaster can be expected. One may well experiment with stepping or even hopping the *unisono* opening tutti of the D minor harpsichord concerto (Example 4.2; and see Example 3.2 above).

What actually happens at the moment of changing note values? If one is walking, hopping, or tapping in the case of a progression from fast to slow, at what point does one become aware of the change in rate of speed? It is with the second of the slower notes because with the first of them it has not yet become apparent that one is going to

Example 4.2 D minor Harpsichord Concerto

slow down. (See Example 4.7.) It is only after the second that one becomes aware of the change in speed. But the second of the slower notes will always need preparation by a tacit subdivision of the first slow note which also serves to insure the accuracy of the metrical relationships. Yet any overt subdivision of the first slow note removes its effectiveness as a slow note in relation to the preceding fast notes. If one were running across the room in fast sixteenth notes and wanted to reduce them to eighths or quarters, something would have to happen between the first and second of the slower notes. The brakes would have to be put on while preparing the second of the slower notes, or, on the momentum generated by the fast notes, one would go flying through the wall, or, less disastrously, through the intended rhythmic pattern. This occurrence of slow notes after fast notes always needs to be looked at, in order to determine whether it has an expressive significance or whether it is being overriden by other musical elements. A great deal of the feel of that moment depends on the degree of activity that has been generated in the preceding fast notes. If the activity is slight, the braking action is also going to be slight. If, however, it is very great, then usually the composer will have underlined the change into slow note values with some device of melodic contour or of harmonic intensification that will give it strength. In an otherwise uneventful diatonic progression it makes very little sense to have such dramatic changes unless they are supported by other musical elements, such as salient melodic contours or increased dissonance. Any progression from fast to slow implies a diminution of momentum. Everything that is in a state of otherwise uninterrupted momentum, any movement formed from one initial impulse, constitutes in the rhythmic sense an indivisible unity. This unity is lost only when a completely new impulse, and consequently a new spurt of momentum, is introduced. But small renewals of energy can very well be subordinated to a prime launching of momentum in such a way that they will be embraced under the curve of a larger gesture. When complex muscles are involved in any movement, the organism is given a dominating signal that controls all smaller signals. This domination of an initial signal over subsequent smaller signals is essential in creating the coherence of what we will later describe as a rhythmic phrase. By and large, the progression from fast to slow guarantees a certain kind of coherence which can be broken only by the influence of other musical elements.

The change from slow to fast is quite a different matter, because a different kind of preparation is necessary in order to bring an impulse into being that will create the momentum that underlies any kind of activity. One of the most frightening things that can be inflicted on anyone is to ask him to put his hand on a table or on the arm of a chair without making any preparation whatsoever for any subsequent movement, and then to lift his hand. Without preparation, any attempt to lift the hand is bound to fail. As in a nightmare, one is frozen into immobility. Since the beginning of any kind of activity needs a preparation, there must be time for that preparation. This does not exclude the possibility of preparing one bit of movement while another is still being executed. If the units of the sequence—preparation, activity, preparation, activity—were to be completely separated, our movements would have no continuity whatever. In going from slower to faster notes one is setting something new into activity. Those moments of preparing for activity—of making the beginning of activity clear not only to oneself and to the listener but also to colleagues in ensemble playing—often express themselves in terms of an articulation, or a momentary cessation of sound immediately before the new activity, namely, before the first of the new faster notes.

One must divest oneself of any habit of overtly subdividing long notes. The long note that is subdivided takes on some of the character of faster notes, and if subdivided enough, becomes just as active, thereby losing any differentiation in expression between activity and repose. This is why the exceedingly salutary discipline of walking to music is far more revealing if the actual rhythmic phrase rather than the meter is walked. The meter will show very little about the expressive shape of the music. One might do well here to conjure up the experience of walking a fugue subject, even a simple one like the E major in Book II (Example 4.3), or walking the augmentations in the D-sharp minor Fugue of Book I (Example 4.4), imagining the feel of it in relation to walking the subject at its ordinary rate of speed. Here is a whole world of expressive choreography!

To a certain extent slow notes can be superficially activated by trills, or by changing notes, or by any kind of figure that revolves around the main note. Very often fast notes, if they fall into groups that outline slower notes, will behave merely like animations of slower notes, thus sacrificing some of their inherent character to the progression established by the slower notes which they outline. Many sequential figures fall into this category. In most Western music there are usually several dimensions, several proportions operating at the

Example 4.3 Fugue E major, II

Example 4.4 Fugue D-sharp minor, I

same time. Most rhythmic figures need to be heard at several different simultaneous rates of speed. It is useless to try to read the meaning of a piece from the superficial picture of the note values. One must search behind the written note values for harmonic rhythms and for the rhythms of those simple contours that underlie melodic decorations. A progression from short to long can be quite a drastic event if it happens only once, but if it happens repeatedly it makes itself into a larger phrase in which it is hardly possible to regard the subsequent short notes as creating a new impulse. If one tries walking such a figure or hopping it, one will find that the impulse necessary to maintain such a progression for any length of time comes from much further back than the ostensible renewal of activity with each short note, namely, from before the first short note that began the phrase.

In the context of momentum, the concept of rhythmic direction becomes fairly clear. As long as momentum is under way, one is going somewhere. It may not be a spatial direction; it may only be a progression from activity into repose. In this sense upbeats lead to downbeats or, irrespective of the meter, upbeat portions of musical phrases lead to downbeat portions.

A rather complicated subject such as that of the B-flat minor Fugue of Book II might be conceived in the following manner, regardless of its metrical notation (Example 4.5). Measure 1 presents an upbeat, measure 2 an afterbeat; measure 3 is a kind of composite upbeat to the first beat of measure 4, to which a second beat forms a kind of decorated afterbeat, which is followed after a rest by a further upbeat. Fast notes in any given figuration can better be under-

stood if one asks where they are coming from and where they are
going. The qualities of rhythm in relation to imaginary movement
can be summed up in three short words: when, where, how.

The way in which we manipulate musical impulses is no different
from the way in which we manipulate our bodies and our spans of
attention. We can produce a large impulse that will span any number
of subsidiary impulses, such as the configurations of melody. These
impulses are formed rather like a tree. The main impulse is the trunk,
so strong in outline that one knows it is a tree and not just a mass of
underbrush. The subsidiary impulses are the branches and so on down
to the leaves. This is so characteristic of the language of form that I
hardly need to insist on it. It is a grammar of the dance and the visual
arts, like that of the construction of sentences and phrases. In any
complete sentence, the subject and predicate are the tree from which
sprout the branches of qualifying adverbs and adjectives that in turn
support less important words down to the little trills and mordents
performed by the leaves and buds and flowers.

There are many intermediate stages between fast and slow notes,
and many variations on them. A dancer, without moving from place,
can add vitality to his stance with a slight movement of an extremity.
Similarly, a long note may preserve its basic function of length even
when it is decorated into a trill or into a series of changing notes. A
group of fast notes on the other hand may become no more than a
smear, which then becomes assimilated as a single note. We have all

Example 4.5 Fugue B-flat minor, II

sometimes heard a passage played so fast that it actually sounds
sluggish because we can no longer hear the movement of the active
parts of the measure. How much of the active detail we are able to
hear is a question of focus. A photographic image can be projected
in or out of focus. Some painters paint minutely every single leaf on
a tree, and others simply paint blobs of color. Similarly we can choose
the degree of focus that we want on a piece of music or on its component elements, harmonic, melodic, or rhythmic. Our choice will
depend on the relative importance we attach to the details or to the
main outline. This choice accounts for most of the manifold differences that are possible in interpretations.

The Formation of Rhythmic Groupings, or Rhythmic Syllables

The progression of impulse through momentum to repose forms
rhythmic groupings, which for lack of a better terminology I call
syllables. They do not behave, however, in the same way as verbal
syllables, and they are often subject to modification by other musical
dimensions. Unless otherwise modified by melodic or harmonic influences, such a syllable embodies a progression from fast to slow,
from activity toward repose. The next syllable is formed when it
becomes necessary to make a new impulse. In the examples in this
chapter, I have used square brackets ⌐¬ or ⌐¬ to mark the beginnings and ends of rhythmic syllables, and occasionally horizontal
lines connecting them: ⌐ or ⌐ . A subsidiary syllabization is indicated by a vertical stroke attached to the horizontal line: ⌐⌐ or ⌐⌐ .
These markings do not necessarily have the same function as those
suggested for melodic articulation in chapter 3. Measures 1–5 of the
Fugue in B-flat major from Book I can be seen to be composed only
of three syllables (Example 4.6). We shall see cases of the enchainment of small fragments that do not necessarily separate themselves
by new impulses (see Example 4.12) but are propelled by renewal
of an initial basic impulse that has already been given. In the Fugue
in B-flat major of Book I, the first debatable syllabic division occurs
between measures 7 and 8, but the sixteenths are merely a decoration of a movement in continuous eighths that runs from the second
beat of measure 7 to the first beat of measure 9.

   In the D minor Fugue of Book II, the change from fast to slower-

Example 4.6   Fugue B-flat major, I

moving notes appears to be clearly supported by the contours of the melodic line, namely, by the leap of the fourth in the second half of measure 1 (Example 4.7). But the rhythmic continuity running from fast to slow motion makes it debatable whether the slower motion established on the second eighth note of measure 1 constitutes a syllable separate from what preceded it. Between the G and F of measure 2 and in corresponding passages, there is a harmonic resolution, which coincides with the beginning of a new rhythmic syllable after the syncopation on the G. Because this harmonic resolution coincides with a new syllable, I would not wish to play a complete legato earlier in this theme, since it would render any articulation of the new syllable excessively conspicuous. (In order to ensure clarity and good ensemble with other moving parts, most good chamber-music players would prefer to interpret the tied-over eighth note on the G as the equivalent of a rest whose duration depends on the manner in which it prepares what follows.) If measures 1 and 2 were to be played in a slight non-legato, their momentum would be car-

Example 4.7   Fugue D minor, II

ried over the tied syncopation on G into the subsequent syllable that
begins with the resolution on F, and any articulation at this point
would not risk breaking up the total phrase. But we should not over-
look the fact that the notated version of this fugue subject is already
a decoration of a subject in simpler form. The whole fugue can be
played substituting even sixteenths for the triplet decoration (Example 4.8) or it can be reduced still further to even eighth notes
throughout (Example 4.9).

The A major Fugue of Book II (Example 4.10) offers an unusually
fascinating set of syllables formed by wildly irregular shapes that
impose themselves on the basic meter in such fashion that the bar
lines might well be ignored. We have spoken of the undesirability of
subdividing longer notes, but when such longer notes are formed by
syncopations, an accentuation on the syncopation can often be even
more undesirable than subdividing. Rather, it is the function of the
other moving parts to make the syncopation clear. In most cases the
syncopation is best expressed by the faster motion of the notes preceding it in the same voice, and by the articulation separating the
syncopated note from the resumption of a faster movement (Example 4.11; see also Example 4.2).

Because of the irregular length of its syllables, composed sometimes of slow-moving notes and sometimes of long waves of eighth
notes, the F-sharp minor Fugue of Book I (Example 4.12) rewards
study. The demarcation of some syllables might be considered debatable, as in measure 5 where the resolution of F-sharp to E-sharp
precludes any excessive articulation. But in measure 7 a chain of

Example 4.8 Fugue D minor, II, rhythmic reduction

Example 4.9 Fugue D minor, II, with further rhythmic reduction

Example 4.10 Fugue A major, II

new upbeats begins that derives a certain importance from its trans-
ference of momentum to what follows.

A look at the Fugue in G minor in Book I will demonstrate some
further examples of rhythmic syllabization (Example 4.13.) In measure 1 there is only one syllable, but in measure 2 we find a composite syllable which is merely an activation of the rhythm of the
first syllable. Since this activation is later used to form a sequence,
I would prefer a continuous detaché to breaking it up into the smallest groups. So from the beginning of the subject's first entrance in
this fugue we have one syllable, then a composite syllable, and then
another composite syllable (measures 1–3). In fact, with the passing
notes taken out, this whole fugue could be played in eighths and
quarters (Example 4.14).

The D major Fugue of Book II is very consistent in its treatment
(Example 4.15). There is an afterbeat on the C-sharp in measure 4
that inverts the one in measure 2, but both are derived from the

Example 4.11 Fugue D-sharp minor, I

Example 4.12 Fugue F-sharp minor, I

Example 4.13 Fugue G minor, I

Example 4.14 Fugue G minor, I, rhythmic reduction

Example 4.15 Fugue D major, II

Example 4.16 Fugue D major, II

afterbeat in measure 1. The whole piece in fact is built on a series of upbeats and afterbeats and their enchainment can be traced backward from the end of the piece as in Example 4.16.

Were it desirable, which here it is not, a slight slowing down of upbeats could be used to produce a gradual ritard. But one can slow down such a rhythmic figure only by making use of a melodic contour such as the fourth in this case, or by taking advantage of a dissonance.

In the Fugue in B-flat major of Book II, the nature of the thematic material might lead to the introduction of a greater number of syllables than would its purely rhythmic structure (Example 4.17). In a preliminary way, I would indicate only the changes from slow into faster movement. But in order to carry out the melodic pattern, one might want to articulate the fourth in measures 2 and 3 and in other measures further on. In measure 27 in the bass the new pickup of speed occurs on the first eighth (Example 4.18), but that eighth actually is the end of what came before; thematically the new phrase really begins with the second eighth. But perhaps one of the reasons that both rhythmically and melodically the articulation in this piece has a tendency to be so bland is that the eighth notes are merely elaborations of a basic movement in quarter notes (Example 4.19). This fugue played only in quarter notes appears to yield a kind of minuet of which the notated version is merely a thematically consistent *double*.

Rhythmic Polyphony

For an experiment in rhythmic polyphony, one might take the C minor Fugue in Book I (see Example 3.2) and, assigning each voice to a different person, constitute a percussion section of tapping pencils. The introduction of any kind of artificial accents or any accentuation of downbeats should be avoided. For the moment one might do well to act as if the piece had no bar lines.

Example 4.17 Fugue B-flat major, II

Example 4.18 Fugue B-flat major, II

Example 4.19 Fugue B-flat major, II

In the overlapping interaction of rhythmic syllables one discovers the transfers of momentum that take place. In good ensemble playing, any break into faster motion is likely to be preceded by at least a slight articulation, so that the other player knows where one is, so that he has his chance of setting off a new burst of motion in the same way, and so that there can be a genuine give and take among voices and among players. It is very hard to play ensemble with someone who fails to articulate.

But if the player who does not articulate is difficult to deal with, equally troublesome is that player who lets himself be carried away by the momentum of fast notes within a given rhythmic syllable in disregard of what is happening in the other parts. Sometimes this

can happen even when one is playing alone. When the running conjunct figure appears in the C-sharp minor Fugue of Book I (Example
4.20) or in the F-sharp minor Fugue of Book II (Example 4.21), it
is difficult to keep from being swept into a slightly more fluid tempo
because of the very nature of the continuous diatonic faster movement. The best way in which one can apply the brakes is to vocalize
all the fast notes and to extract from the melodic contour the maximum amount of braking power. One can always catch oneself at the
moment of any interruption of diatonic motion, or when there is any
kind of dissonance on which to lean.

No one who has ever played ensemble needs to be told that the
guiding role is always played by the smallest note values, by the
person who has the upbeats and the subdivisions of the beat. With a
downbeat one cannot influence anyone. But a sensitive second vio-

Example 4.20 Fugue C-sharp minor, I

Example 4.21 Fugue F-sharp minor, II

linist in a quartet, simply by the way he plays his offbeats in the accompanying parts, can extract from the first violinist the most heavenly phrasing imaginable. It is the skillful accompanist who has led many singers to perform miracles.

In my Scarlatti preface I spoke of rhythmic polyphony in the following terms:

> In all good ensemble playing, rhythmic polyphony is derived from different rates of speed in different voices, and from non-simultaneous occurrence of accents and impulses.
>
> Nothing will more effectively kill rhythmic polyphony in performance than simultaneous accents in all parts, subdivision of long notes which deprives them of their relative repose, and excessive subordination of irregular movement of note values to the regular movement of the basic pulse.
>
> A rhythmic influence may be exerted by one voice on another not only through those notes which subdivide the beat, but also and principally through the enchainment of impulses from active upbeats. [See Example 4.16.]

Rhythm and Imaginary Movement

Hitherto we have been preoccupied mainly with the structural aspects of rhythm, but it is now necessary to discuss some of the means of endowing rhythm with character. Unless the notes of a melody have been transmuted in terms of vocal experience, they can be played entirely correctly and yet fail to sing. Similarly, rhythm only comes to life through transmutation into imaginary movement. One can play a rhythm perfectly correctly, one can articulate it at all the right places, one can give it all the right punctuations, and yet fail to endow it with a character of its own. We have a tendency to feel legato with our innards and detaché with our extremities. We represent the songful and the lyrical and the subcutaneous with legato, and the active, the dance element, the locomotive with non-legato in movements that correspond to the necessarily articulated motions that we make in order to dance or run or leap.

It is important not only where one goes *from*, and where one goes *to*, and *when*, but especially *how*. To a considerable degree intervals are allied with the *how* of rhythmic treatment. Conjunct motion is patently weaker and less active than disjunct. The tendency of conjunct intervals to fuse into a larger unit of continuous and unrenewed momentum often brings them close to the equivalent of a long note and allies them with the relative passivity of legato. This means that sources of strength and emphasis are to be sought in disjunct intervals, which regenerate activity and which in their alliance with the detaché that is natural to them serve to set off momentum.

For purposes of achieving rhythmic characterization, legato is of little use. With a legato one cannot leap, one can only slide. One cannot even walk to a legato; one can only glide. Legato is not to be relied on if one wants to generate energy. Of course, there are elements inside a legato that can be of help, such as dynamics and inflection of harmonic intensities. But in the course of a rhythmic syllable or a rhythmic phrase, legato has a tendency to weaken momentum. If diminishing aggressiveness is to be expressed, or a slackening of energy, then the detaché can be lengthened and carried toward the flabbiness of a legato. Tonal relations can be expressed in this way, as for example in certain episodes of the G minor and B-flat minor Fugues of Book II. I may have no dynamics at my disposal, or I may not choose to use them, and the basic articulation is determined by the thematic material. But by letting the articulation become soft and gummy, I can express the collapse into a juicy major or the relaxation of a long-postponed arrival into the home tonality.

In recent years I have become much more conscious than ever before of the possibilities of shading through articulation. Again and again in dealing with Book II of the *WTC*, I have felt perfectly content to work in terms of the harpsichord's lack of dynamics. A few years before, I would have been most desperately missing the clavichord and all its capacities for nuance. The experience of discovering much more clearly the relationship between articulation and rhythm has revealed a set of possibilities of which I was hitherto not entirely conscious.

Earlier I alluded to the possibility of embracing a whole series of impulses and motions within the momentum generated by a larger movement. This is precisely what a great actor does when he makes a long slow gesture that fills an entire stage. Anyone who has known the Kabuki theater of Japan will have seen the richest examples of that kind of eloquence that I can imagine. But this is exactly what a musician does if he wants to lend cohesiveness to a long phrase. He finds a gesture, an inward impulse, that is so compelling that it will dominate the span of the phrase and hold it together.

Summary of Essential Rhythmic Relationships and Means of Expression

Let me sum up the essential elements with which we have been dealing: measurement, pulse, differentiation, continuity and discontinuity, activity and repose, impulse, momentum, direction, character of movement, and the means within the keyboard of expressing all these—that is, articulation and phrasing, dynamics and accent, agogics, preparations, and above all the relation of every element to every other one within the infinite variety of possibilities.

CHAPTER V.

The Harmonic Approach

BACH'S HARMONIC STYLE · CHARACTERISTICS OF VERTICAL COMBI-
NATIONS OF SOUND · THE CHORDS OF THOROUGHBASS—THEIR CLAS-
SIFICATION AND HIERARCHY · CHORDS AND THEIR COMPONENTS IN
THE CONTEXT OF TONALITY · HARMONIC INTENSITY (OR ACTIV-
ITY)—ITS DEGREES AND DISTRIBUTION · DIAGONAL HARMONIC RE-
LATIONSHIPS · ESSENTIAL HARMONIC AND TONAL PROGRESSIONS AND
THE VARYING DEGREES OF THEIR ELABORATION · TONAL STRUC-
TURE—THE ORIENTATION OF A PIECE AS A WHOLE · THE VOCAL
SENSE OF HARMONY · THE INNER HARMONIC EAR—DISCIPLINES IN
SHARPENING ITS PERCEPTIONS · THE EXPRESSION ON KEYBOARD IN-
STRUMENTS OF HARMONY AND HARMONIC INTENSITIES

Bach's Harmonic Style

Harmony is a musical phenomenon that is almost exclusive to the
western hemisphere. As a language and as a means of structure, it
is probably the most fluid of the three main dimensions of music and
the one that is least translatable into other media. Beginning as a
kind of by-product of polyphony, harmony became, by the age of
thoroughbass, a structural element that was ultimately extended into
the far-flung spans of tonality that we know from the nineteenth
century.

Contrary to the legend that Bach is first and foremost a master of
linear counterpoint, he might well be considered primarily a har-
monist. Indeed, the creative germ of any Bach composition is to be
found in its harmonic and tonal substructure. Unlike most so-called
Baroque music, Bach's music is in fact based on a characteristically

Baroque technique of elaborating simple forms into a labyrinth of complexities, for which parallels can easily be found in the architecture of a Bernini or a Balthasar Neumann, or in the complex verbal constructions of Milton's *Paradise Lost*.

Skillful as Bach is in overlaying his harmonic skeleton with decorations and with what almost looks like independent linear counterpoint, the elements that determine the length and fundamental proportions of a Bach piece are usually to be traced to the harmonic and tonal substructure. Bach's bass-dominated harmony is closely knit together by the strong pull of horizontal voice-leading. Quite foreign to Bach is Scarlatti's leaping from point to point of tonality, with much less overt horizontal connection. The ambiguities of the *Chromatic Fantasy*, with its enharmonic changes and bizarre turns of tonality, are allied more with the experiments of the seventeenth century than with those of the nineteenth. Though Bach in the *WTC* uses all the twenty-four major and minor tonalities, he makes but little use of their potential modulatory range in shaping the tonal structure of an individual piece. Much as he may stretch its bounds, Bach's harmony is firmly rooted in the language of thoroughbass. It is to C. P. E. Bach, in his fantasies and rondos, that one has to turn to hear the genuine prophet.

Characteristics of Vertical Combinations of Sound

The terminology of harmony that has been widely accepted for the past two centuries is superficially and perhaps deceptively clear, especially because it is well-nigh impossible to separate the functions of harmony from those of tonality. The terminology that I devised for the chapter on harmony in my *Domenico Scarlatti* has more than once been questioned—first by Paul Hindemith, to whom I showed a draft of that chapter, and later by my German translator—for its failure to draw a clear distinction between the functions of harmony and those of tonality, especially in terms of prevailing Germanic usage. Nevertheless I have retained it because I feel that the performer is inevitably affected by a mixture of the two functions.

Many of us who have submitted to so-called courses in harmony have had difficulty in associating with real music the mere labeling of chords or the piecing together of exercises for blue-penciling and pounding out on a chalk-dusty classroom piano. One has the impression that the usual harmony exercises, negotiable as they are by intelligent deaf mutes, have very little to do with the workings of the human ear, much less with human musical emotion. Fortunately, choral singing can supplement, as it did for me, what for lack of time and favorable circumstances is seldom adequately pursued in harmony classes. Furthermore, one can learn from the clavichord, more than from any other keyboard instrument, that nothing that is not musical can be expected to make any sense, especially harmonic sense. Beyond the subjective revelations afforded by choral singing and the intimacy of the clavichord, the experience of continuo playing can provide a more objective insight into the many levels on which harmony functions in the formation of musical structures. It is no accident that the French conservatories link continuo playing, transposition, and orchestral score reading at the piano in something that they call *accompagnement*. All these activities presuppose a liberation from the literal approach to the musical notation in that they demand an exercise of musical thought and selectivity in choosing which notes to play and which to leave out. One might say, double entendre aside, that one develops the habit of assessing the basic anatomical conformations of any casually encountered piece of music by divesting it in imagination of its melodic and harmonic decorations and of the instrumental colors in which it is clothed.

Even though the hierarchy of consonance and dissonance has traditionally been well established, we all can profit from any exercise that leads us to reexamine the nature of vertical harmonic intervals and the often unpredictable ways in which they affect us. One might evaluate them in terms of intensity or activity. The relative dissonant content of two-voice intervals has long been associated with the series of overtones obtained by dividing the vibrating string in successive halves, with the result that the greatest degree of dissonance corresponds in general to the upper notes of the overtone series. More complex vertical combinations of tones have been assessed with a precision which does not always account for their effect upon the human ear and voice in terms of their function in real music. One of the most lucid of recent presentations of the hierarchy of consonance and dissonance is to be found in Paul Hindemith's *Craft of Musical Composition*, where a table is provided of chord groups ranging from quiet harmlessness to the intense agitation of tone clusters.[1] These receive further explanations throughout the book and especially in the chapter on harmonic fluctuation. But the relationships of these combinations of sounds are so much affected by the uses to which they are put within a musical composition that in actuality the ear is a better judge of their function than the mind. Especially when they are adapted to the tempered scale, we must hear their function in terms of what our musical imagination and our accumulated experience have taught us to expect. This gives all the more reason for saying that function, experience, and imagination count for more on any keyboard instrument than the actual sounds it emits.

The Chords of Thoroughbass—Their Classification and Hierarchy

The classifications used in the average eighteenth-century manual of thoroughbass provide the most convenient access to Bach's harmony. From treatise to treatise, they undergo very little change and there is ample evidence that Bach thought in their terms. Their nomenclature, which is based on the distance of the various intervals from the bass, serves to emphasize the supreme importance of the bass in a supremely tonal music.

The usual treatise leads the beginner from simple triads to chords of the sixth; then to 6/4 and 6/5 chords; to seventh chords in all keys and degrees of the scale; to ninths; and to further combinations formed by suspensions and requiring preparation and resolution. Any of these chords can be said to have a specific content of intensity, which, however, is subject to the influence of tonality. The language of thoroughbass cannot be conceived as independent of its context in tonality.

The relation of chords to each other should not be assessed without the relation of their component notes to the bass. In a 6/4 chord such as Example 5.1a, the sixth is more consonant than the fourth, as is also the third between the two upper voices. But in a 6/4/2 chord such as Example 5.1b, the second and the augmented fourth are dissonant with the bass in contrast with the blandness of the sixth

1. Hindemith, Paul: *The Craft of Musical Composition, Book I.* New York [1942].

Example 5.1 Consonance and dissonance in chords

and of the thirds between the top three voices. It would be very difficult to disassociate the values of component parts of chords from their inevitable behavior within the framework of horizontal part-writing and of tonality. According to the prevailing nineteenth-century classification of chords, we are taught that the 6/3 chord with its sounding bass on the fourth degree of the scale is an inversion of a 5/3 chord on the second degree, whereas in reality it is merely a changing function of a 5/3 chord on the fourth degree (Example 5.2a), as is also its closely related transformation into a 6/5 chord on the same degree where both the fifth and the sixth are simultaneously sounding and just as frequently associated in cadential formulas with the subdominant (Example 5.2b). In analyzing Bach's harmony, it is preferable to label chords in terms of eighteenth-century figured bass, without adding the Roman numerals that are customary to nineteenth- and twentieth-century harmony treatises. These are better reserved for indicating areas of tonality in terms of the piece as a whole.

The levels of harmonic intensity are affected by many influences. Harmony has a way of spilling over into its surroundings. Even when every chord has been identified, as well as every component note and every decoration, the total effect of the harmony in the context of a piece is still far from having been explained. But, as with melody, there is one sure method, and that is the vocal approach, either

Example 5.2 Subdominant function of 6/3 and 6/5 chords

real or imaginary. It will usually indicate a great deal more than any amount of theorizing.

Let us take the C major Prelude from Book I as it would be sung when reduced to its fundamental five parts and if every part were treated as a vocal line in the context of the fluctuating harmonic intensity it can reflect. A very simple way of examining one's feeling for the harmony of a given passage is to take pairs of successive chords and determine which within the context is more and which less intense (Example 5.3). About the first two measures of this prelude there can be no doubt. But the difference between the harmonies of measures 2–3 is not as great, whereas between measures 3–4 there can be no equivocation. It is a useful exercise to go on comparing pairs of measures throughout the piece.

Chords and Their Components in the Context of Tonality

More important than the mere classification of chords is the perception of their differentiation. We are taught that some chords move in certain directions, that certain intervals move up or down, all of the stock progressions we learn in harmony class. But we do not always assess the relative activity, that is, the relative degrees of intensity of what is going on, in the harmonic and tonal dimensions of a piece. We know, but do not always bother to feel, that no two chords in a piece are alike.

In the varying context of tonality, even identical chords can change their function. Depending on its relation to the tonal context, the active content of the harmony will vary. At moments of borrowing from foreign keys or at moments of actual modulation, there will always be an increase in the activity of certain chords.

Example 5.3 Prelude C major, I, harmonic outline

The concept of harmonic shape is also closely allied with tonality, and it is scarcely necessary to indicate the simplest possible harmonic shape, that of tonic-dominant-tonic. This is the irreducible minimum on which a piece can be composed, namely, a beginning, middle, and end, and many pieces are nothing but expansions and elaborations of this scheme.

Bach's cadences have characteristics that are misunderstood by those performers who taper them off into a diminuendo or a relaxation that comes far too soon. The final establishment of the dominant forms the center of gravity of a Bach cadence. If tapered off too soon to a dying close, it can be seriously weakened. One often has to be careful not to relax until the very moment of arriving at the tonic. (See Example 5.4.) In a Bach phrase it is difficult to relax convincingly while still on a dominant or in an area that is engaged in reinforcing the dominant.

Shaping a phrase in terms of the dosage and disposition of disso-

Example 5.4 Prelude B major, I

nance is a characteristic procedure of Bach. It shows in a particularly conspicuous way in his recitatives, where he often contrives to put the strongest harmonic intensity on a key word. (This makes the problem of translation all the greater because of the difference between German and English word order.) Bach's treatment of recitative finds a parallel in the Prelude in E-flat minor of Book I. Irrespective of the melodic context, the mere diagram of relative harmonic intensities has a plausible shape (Example 5.5).

Accounting for the dissonant content of vertical chords in terms of the harmonic series or by calculating the sum of dissonance, as some theorists have done, often eliminates any distinction between a chord and its so-called inversion. If sixth chords are given the same evaluation as root-position chords, very little reflection is obtained of their true function. Perhaps some of the leveling process that has taken place in harmony since the nineteenth century is the result of this theory of chord inversions. This leveling process is reflected even in the writings and behavior of such sensitive musicians as Walter Piston[2] and Arnold Schönberg[3] when they attempted to account for harmonic phenomena in terms of the theory of chord inversion. Schönberg, especially, in his *Harmonielehre* goes to considerable lengths to point out what his classification does not adequately explain. But for all of us, the watchword is *Listen*.

Harmonic Intensity (or Activity)—Its Degrees and Distribution

In connection with harmony, I often use the terms *active* and *passive*. If we go back to the beginning of the C major Prelude of Book I (see Example 5.3), it is clear that we have a tonic which is relatively passive. But from measure 2 we are actively moving, at least as far as measure 4. An aggregation of notes sounding simultaneously has a kind of total effect, but the behavior of its component tones varies in character. If we examine the individual voices of this prelude, we first find that the relatively inactive bass C of measure 1 becomes active in measure 2 because of the downward pull created by the necessity of resolving into the B of measure 3 the dissonance

2. Piston, Walter: *Harmony*. New York, 1941.
3. Schönberg, Arnold: *Harmonielehre*. Leipzig-Wien, 1911.

Example 5.5 Prelude E-flat minor, I, harmonic reduction

against the doubled Ds of tenor and second soprano. Another active interval of measure 2 is the F of the soprano which pulls downward to its resolution in measure 4 on E, which itself is relatively inactive. As the foregoing examples suggest, it is not difficult to distinguish the relative degrees of activity and passivity in the component notes of chords, yet many performers fail to do so. Too often one hears a player attempting to extract an active expressivity from a note that is inherently passive. It resembles an actor or a singer reciting a text in a foreign language of which he does not understand the parts of speech.

We have already drawn from the C major Prelude the implication that it gives its own indications for dynamics. If one has any understanding of the harmonic functioning of this piece, there is no necessity for being told where to make a crescendo and where a diminuendo, where to play piano and where forte. Such indications are like giving literate adults directions for pronouncing their native language. After all, we are dealing with a harmonic language which is perfectly established and self-evident to those who understand its pronunciation and syntax. Just as there is a natural inflection of melodic intervals, so there is a natural inflection of harmony. This can be qualified by the context, or even by the superposition of dynamics as a kind of additional dimension. But in both cases natural inflection is fundamental and, as a point of departure, absolutely essential to any truly intelligent performance.

It should be obvious that chords in a well-made piece of music function in relation to each other and that their inflection is influenced by a sense of the direction in which they are going, by a sense that they or their components are moving toward a greater or lesser activity. Thus in our C major Prelude, the chords repeated in the second half of every measure are different from those in the first half, the difference depending on where they are going. For instance, in the second half of the very first measure, the C major chord is no longer as passive as it was in the first half, for it is preparing the increase of activity that takes place in the first half of measure 2. But the second halves of measure 2 and 3 are preparing diminutions of activity into the first halves of the succeeding measures. Just as in an isolated melody one interval prepares another, in harmony a chord or its components prepare what follows.

Diagonal Harmonic Relationships

It should be observed that in our apprehension of harmony we have a kind of built-in damper pedal such that we do not cut off a given harmony at the time it ostensibly ceases, but go on reacting to it. But as we have already seen, we are also sluggish enough to need some kind of preparation for that which is to come. This is why the preparation of one harmony by another can involve diagonal relationships with what follows. In these diagonal relationships cross relations are the most obvious. Hearing the C-sharp in relation to the G that is coming will lend intensity to the passage in Example 5.6a. Very often intensities of dissonance can be introduced where their intervals are not simultaneously present, as in Example 5.6b, where both F-sharp and D can be played in relation to the following G-sharp, or the E and the G-sharp in relation to the preceding D.

Example 5.6 Diagonal relationships

Diagonal relationships occur not only in relation to what is coming but also in relation to what has already sounded. In the first measure of the A minor Prelude I (see Example 6.1), the B in the soprano can be played in relation to the preceding A to give a momentary quiver of intensity, like the G-sharp of the changing notes later in the measure. In measure 4, in order to avoid an excessive relaxation, the second E-natural could be played in relation to D-sharp. In this case it is not particularly desirable. However, diagonal relationships of dissonance offer the possibility of generating a certain amount of intensity even in the blandest of harmonic progressions, whether or not one chooses to profit by them. (See Example 5.7.)

Allied with what I call diagonal relationships are those devices that can be used to evoke the continuing presence of a note that has not sustained itself (Example 5.8), or even to conjure up a note that

Example 5.7 Further diagonal relationships

Example 5.8 Prelude B minor, I

is not actually sounding (like many of the unstated bass parts in Bach's pieces for unaccompanied violin). The B minor Prelude of Book I is full of dissonances created by suspensions on notes that on a keyed stringed instrument may well have ceased to sound by the time the greatest degree of dissonance is arrived at. Since one is powerless to do anything with those notes themselves, their dissonant content can only be expressed by the manner in which one plays the moving parts in other voices. In measure 1, the first suspension in the alto on B, and to a certain extent its preparation on F-sharp, can be brought out by using the dissonant passing note on C-sharp in the bass. E, the fourth bass note in this measure, is a perfectly bland consonance unless one chooses to hear it in relation to the alto F-sharp. Logically, the ensuing bass G-sharp would undergo a similar treatment in relation to the soprano entrance, but since it anticipates the alto G-sharp of measure 2, its treatment needs to be slightly different, in fact a kind of compromise. However, if one simply plays the notes in a more or less mechanical fashion on a non-sustaining keyed instrument, it will be difficult even to hear that the piece is in three voices.

Essential Harmonic and Tonal Progressions and the Varying Degrees of Their Elaboration

Composition in Bach's time, and most keyboard instruction, began with thoroughbass. Treatises such as those of Niedt[4] (used by Bach himself), Mattheson,[5] and Heinichen[6] expounded the manipulation of basic chords and sequences, and the progressive degrees of their modification through passing notes, changing notes, and motivic figuration in ways that are all exemplified in the preludes of the *WTC*.

An example of the effect of changing notes on a simple harmonic skeleton can be found in the C minor Prelude of Book I. If one strips the piece of all its changing notes and then reintroduces them, one discovers how they lend a kind of shimmer to the basic harmony (Example 5.9). In the F major prelude of Book II, a spate of melodic

4. Niedt, F. E.: *Musicalishe Handleitung oder Gründlicher Unterricht* . . . Hamburg, 1700.
5. Mattheson, Johann: *Grosse General-Bass-Schule*. Hamburg, 1731.
6. Heinichen, J. D.: *Der General-Bass in der Composition* . . . Dresden, 1728.

Example 5.9 Prelude C minor, I, harmonic reduction

decoration is used to pour a great wash of sound over the fundamental harmony.

The figuration imposed on the simple harmonic structure may be motivic, as in the Preludes in D major and B major of Book I, or even imitative as in the aforementioned Prelude in B minor of Book I; or it may make use of double counterpoint as in the A minor of Book II.

Beyond a reduction to its simplest harmonic skeleton (see Example 5.5), the E-flat minor Prelude of Book I can benefit by the extraction of every bit of dissonance from the smallest notes of the melodic decoration as heard against the prevailing harmony. (See Example 5.10.) Levels of expressivity reveal themselves that might have escaped attention had not the inner ear been directed to them. Hearing the superficial decoration not only in relation to what is there but also to what is not there, in the sense that it is only implied rather than overtly stated, is particularly necessary in works like the unaccompanied cello suites and violin partitas. Scale passages can

Example 5.10 Prelude E-flat minor, I, rewritten

be heard in two ways, either as successive notes connected only horizontally or as notes bearing a fluctuating relationship to the unstated bass. The opening of the *Chromatic Fantasy* gains richness when heard not merely as a scale passage but in relation to its underlying harmony.

Tonal Structure—The Orientation of a Piece as a Whole

Tonal structure is not as directly apparent to the ear as the relations of chords, and yet it is the larger organization of tonality which makes it possible to construct a big piece, and understanding this is what makes a performance of the piece hold together. Especially where the same thematic material and the same harmonic progressions repeat themselves in various contexts, their principal differentiation occurs in relation to the keys in which they appear, and in turn in the relationship of those keys to the original tonic. Even the finest Schubert and Beethoven piano sonatas can be made to fall apart when the performer fails to sense and make clear the relationships of tonalities. Maintenance of tonal relationships is to a large extent what makes the difference between controlling a big fugue of Bach as a whole, and letting it fall into insufficiently related fragments. Only then can one arch the curve that defines the piece as a whole and keep it from sagging, and with it of course the participation of the hearer.

Some years ago, in the course of restudying Book I of the *WTC* on the clavichord, I undertook some experiments in the hope of finding out why my instinct led me to certain dispositions of dynamics and tone color in performing some of the fugues. I went through all the fugues, plotting areas of tonality while totally disregarding thematic content. In many cases I found substantiation for my instincts. I also found the distribution of thematic material coincided with the distribution of tonal structure.

For an example of the manner in which a performer might orient himself in terms of tonal structure, one might look at the broad outlines of the E major Fugue in Book II. These are most obviously defined by cadences, since a cadence is always a clear confession of tonality, whether fundamental or only temporary. (See Example 5.11.)

Diagram of cadences in E major Fugue (Bk. II)

Measure:	9	16	23	28	35	43
Cadence:	V	vi	ii	V	vi/V	I
	B	c♯	f♯	B	g♯	E

Example 5.11 Fugue E major, II, diagram of cadences

Our first cadence, in dominant B, is to be found in measure 9. After considerable harmonic activity, the next cadence occurs at measure 16 in C-sharp minor, the relative minor. Further activity leads to F-sharp minor in measure 23 and even beyond. Despite the hint of a deceptive cadence in measure 27, the dominant is reached in a kind of half cadence in measure 28 (which should not be given too much emphasis or the piece will fall apart). At measure 35 a full cadence is reached on G-sharp, the relative minor of the dominant. A comparison of the tonalities reached in these cadences with the home tonality of E major will reveal, at least in a primitive way, their relative remoteness and the activity they represent in relation to the home tonality. The relation of the dominant B major with our home tonality is close, but the next tonality, C-sharp minor, the relative minor, is a little further removed. And F-sharp minor, the relative minor of the subdominant, and G-sharp minor, the relative minor of the dominant, will each feel different in relation to the home tonality. But any such assessments must be made directly by the ear through contrasting the actual chords rather than simply taking for granted their verbally stated function.

In most Bach fugues, the continuity is carried unbroken through cadences by horizontal voice-leading which permits no clean-cut vertical break. Even when there are perceptible pauses between sections, the Bach fugue is essentially a one-piece form. This is why changes of registration or of manual introduced into the fugues of the *WTC*, even though they may lend an element of variety to an otherwise unsatisfactory performance, almost invariably disrupt the basic structure. As in his own orchestrations, Bach assures variety by the dropping out or reentry of individual voices. Nothing can destroy the structure of Bach fugues more than the mannerisms of those performers who overemphasize the entrances of subject material at the expense of what they mistakenly conceive as subsidiary

rather than as organic extensions of or oppositions to the basic subject material.

The Vocal Sense of Harmony

If singing can illuminate the nature of a single melodic line, certainly the singing of every voice in a combination of melodic lines
can do even more to reveal the context in terms of harmony and
tonality. No one can be considered competent to play a Bach fugue
who has not sung every line in it. Certainly the first step toward a
comprehension of the harmonic and tonal content of a piece is to
sing its bass line. Those notes that do not sufficiently sustain on a
keyed stringed instrument should be repeated often enough to reveal
their relation to the other parts. While singing a single voice it can
sometimes be useful to reduce the other voices to a kind of harmonic
skeleton like that provided by a simple thoroughbass. One must never
forget that habits induced by instruments can so dull inner hearing
that unless it constantly renews itself it can become the slave rather
than the master of the instrument.

The Inner Harmonic Ear—Disciplines in
Sharpening Its Perceptions

I do not think I ever play a Bach work of any kind without hearing
it in a harmonic context. Even if it appears to be a predominantly
contrapuntal work, even if it is only a two-part invention, my inner
ear hears it dripping with harmony. There is a kind of harmonic
atmosphere from which it gains its life and breath. Without it, it
would shrink to something very insignificant indeed. There is present in everything I play a kind of silent, unwritten continuo. In teaching
I have often supplied a continuo in order to stimulate the imagination
and sensibilities of my pupils. It is hardly to be believed how much
better they play when supported by an added continuo.

I can well recall that it took me years to acquire security in this
kind of hearing. At first it had constantly to be renewed, for my
musical imagination was not strong enough to hold what I was not
physically hearing. I would be obliged to go back to repeating the
long notes that did not hold through, and of course to singing them;
sometimes I would go to the organ to fortify my ear with its sus-

tained sound. In the case of highly decorated keyboard pieces, I would sing for myself the top or middle voice of a theoretical continuo.

Since the bass is our principal guide to the nature of any chord with which we are dealing and to its function within a tonality, identification of the real bass in any given measure will clear up any ambiguities and make possible the focusing of all the neighboring passages around this point of clarification. It is most instructive to cut away from the bass every bit of decoration and every harmonic step that is not absolutely essential until a series of chords has been reached which cannot any further be reduced. Similarly, in studying verbal syntax, one may eliminate from a long and flowery sentence all the qualifying words until one has arrived at its essentials. (An interesting exercise which I occasionally assigned to pupils was the reduction of the first complete sentence [sixteen lines] of Milton's *Paradise Lost* to the minimum number of words essential to that sentence.)

Having reduced the bass to its essential notes, one does well to figure it, and then to realize a continuo over it. It should suffice simply to play it without writing it out, and without at first worrying too much about part-writing. A convincing upper part can merely be given a provisional filling-in of inner parts. The continuo can gradually be elaborated, the decorations of the bass restored, and the part-writing refined until little by little the return to the original written text is consummated.

The Expression on Keyboard Instruments of Harmony and Harmonic Intensities

If I were to be asked how on keyboard instruments harmony and harmonic intensities are to be expressed, I would first talk of dissonance and consonance, of tension and release, and of the pull exerted by tonality, all of which represent various degrees of activity and passivity. If these are genuinely heard and felt by a keyboard player, they will always show in his playing. Even in the case of unskillful players, I have never seen a fully developed musical sensibility entirely fail to transmit itself. Any feeling that is precise and clear is bound to show itself as long as it is not smothered by the interference of bad instrumental habits and editorial misdirections.

Dynamics offer the most immediately obvious way of expressing small nuances, such as the resolutions of dissonances. Connecting anything that belongs together is very easy if done with a dying fall. This still represents an uninterruptible progression of activity into repose. But there are ways of translating into terms of articulation what in the voice might occur through dynamics, change of timbre, or syllabization. Obviously articulation can be used in such a way as to denote which harmonic resolutions are connected with their foregoing dissonances and to denote separations of what is harmonically not connected. The gradation of detaché as a means of denoting varying degrees of activity is as applicable to harmony as it is to melody and rhythm.

The expression of tonal and harmonic shape often works together with a sense of rhythmic direction. The tendency that many performers have to press forward in modulatory passages is a reflection of harmonic and tonal activity. When the harmony is relaxing, there can also be a tendency to relax the forward push. Hence the ritards that coincide with the relaxation afforded by cadences.

In passages permitting arpeggiation, even where there is no possibility of crescendo and diminuendo, one can express the whole gamut of harmonic intensities by increasing or decreasing the speed of arpeggiation of the component chords. In the accompaniment of recitatives and recitative-like passages, there are limitless possibilities of expression, as may be heard in my recordings of the E-flat minor Prelude of Book I. One may note that the arpeggiations, while nearly always differentiated, are constantly striking a balance among the inflection of the harmonies, the expression of the rhythmic curve of the phrase, and the number of notes composing the individual chords. In no way is any uniformity of treatment imposed upon these chords beyond a general adherence to the basic 3/2 pulse. One must never forget that any kind of differentiation lends itself to translation from one medium to another.

The notation of many a Bach piece merely seeks to avoid the complications of the double stemming and ties with which a composer like Couperin underlines the harmonic implications of his basically two-voice writing. Given the nature of much of Bach's harmony, the literal observance of his notation in terms of forbidding the arbitrary holding over of notes, or the use of the damper pedal, is preposterous. The psychological damper pedal is constantly present, or should be present, in all of us. In general, however, holding over of notes by individual fingers is preferable to using the damper pedal for any other purpose than the coloring of sound, since the damper pedal fails to discriminate among individual voices, or among the components of chords.

Like the damper pedal, swell-box dynamics are relatively crude in their functioning. They affect everything at the same time, while leaving insufficient control over individual voices. The orchestral conception of manipulating dynamics is always more satisfactory than the solistic one. One can make an imaginary orchestration in which the basic harmonies are confided to the sustaining wind instruments, as Mozart very often does against the animation of the strings.

The expression of a chord through its preceding context can be exemplified in the B-flat minor Prelude of Book I (Example 5.12), where the intensity of the diminished seventh in measure 22 can be so well prepared by the chords that precede it that once it is reached, it hardly need be played at all. For any important chord, a greater eloquence can always be derived from what precedes it than from the chord itself or from what follows it.

Example 5.12 Prelude B-flat minor, I

CHAPTER VI.

The Interpretive Approach

A Backward Glance

In the course of the melodic, rhythmic, and harmonic approaches
we found ourselves looking for such qualities as uniqueness or plurality, similarity or difference. We measured more and less; we asked
what, when, how, where, whence. We punctuated with and, or, but,
however, nevertheless; we observed or felt activity and passivity,
cohesion and separation, continuity and discontinuity, tension and
relaxation, preparation, impulse, and momentum.

At the so-called esthetic stage, although we are still observers and
not yet doers, we may keenly feel these musical functions and their
effect, but at our own leisure. The performer, however, must incorporate them into his body in direct terms of their operation in time.
He must be prepared for that split-second succession of musical events
to which his physical organism must not only respond but which it
must also bring into being. Everything must be related to everything
else, not intellectually and timelessly, but as a personal experience
to be communicated, an experience that is unique in its own moment
or moments. It is with this immediacy of the moment, with no de-
tached, free time left for observation and contemplation, that the
commitment of the performer begins. It is experience and not obser-

vation that communicates music, and, certainly, providing experience is the job of the performer.

The Approach through the Inner Ear

We have repeatedly said that it is necessary to hear a great deal more than what appears on the notated page, but with that we have still not said enough. Our aim might well be to hear with the ear of the composer. To do this the inner ear must assume a dominating function. How can a composer undergo the rigorous discipline, the dry unrewarding labor, of putting notes on a page which is supposed to flower into music, if his inner ear does not hear that music with an unparalleled intensity? Not only with intensity but with precision! How easy it is for us in a dreamlike state to think that we can remember a piece or a set of ideas. How embarrassing it is in full consciousness to discover that we have only the haziest vague outline instead of what we thought was a precise and fully worked-out conception. For the composer, the discipline of learning to put the right notes in the right place is just such a discipline of converting the hazy vague dream into a finely worked-out composition. It behooves the performer to do the same.

He needs to hear the completeness of which the notes are just an abbreviation. He needs to hear the transitions between notes. He needs to hear the harmonic forces that are at work, both those stated and those that lie behind the indications of the notes. He needs to be aware at all times of the forces and relationships of tonality. (By "aware" I do not mean necessarily consciously aware, but at least subconsciously feeling them.) He must participate in the sense of direction and character of rhythm. And beyond this, having heard the essential qualities of a piece, having reconstructed it from the notes, he must be able to hear precisely what he is going to do with it.

Really to have command of a phrase, really to know that it is going to come out the way one intends it, one must be able to hear it before playing it. Even then for one reason or another, particularly in ensemble music, adjustments may have to be made. But at least the adjustments are made in relation to a point of departure and to a character and set of proportions that have been established for that phrase. In actual performance, of course, the conscious awareness gives way, as it should, to the partially unconscious motor functions of playing. Fortunately, no one has time to think that much. Much that we have talked about functions only in the unconscious, but if we are ever going to feel it, at one time or other it must have entered into our being, if not unconsciously, then consciously.

The inner ear is an enormous aid to the kind of self-hypnotism that a performer needs in order to put and keep himself in the mood for communicating what he has to communicate. It is good to be so filled with the sound of what is to be communicated that it inevitably must come through, even under adverse circumstances. Of course the role of the inner ear can be pushed much too far, or rather it can be pushed further than it should go without the support of the outer ear. We know how atrociously some composers with splendid inner ears can perform on their long-suffering instruments. It is continually necessary for the performer to check the inner ear with the outer ear. One can inwardly hear a piece quite splendidly and yet discover that his instrument is not yielding it at all, or that the instrumental means have not been adopted that will make the piece come off. As a matter of fact, it sometimes takes years of experience to be able to calculate in advance how much the instrument can be counted on to give. Even then one can make mistakes, particularly if one is working in unfamiliar or unfavorable acoustics.

But here is a situation in which the inner ear provides a great deal of help, as I can testify from abundant experience. Because of certain instruments, and because of the large number of exceedingly poor halls in which I have had to play, I have become accustomed to walking out on the stage only to hear a series of sounds that I find absolutely detestable, and having to work for an entire evening as if I were myself enchanted with them, meanwhile hoping that somehow I may convey this enchantment to the hearer, even to those who are placed in the worst seats in the house! At such times there is no comfort like the inner ear for helping a musical conception to carry not only into a strange hall, but by way of a strange instrument. If one is secure in the feel of the basic design, one is much less disconcerted by the caprices of an unfamiliar instrument or by unfavorable surroundings. In other words, one may have to modify the language that one speaks, but at least one knows absolutely clearly what is to be said.

In the recording studio, the inner ear comes into an even more complex set of relations with the outer ear. In the concert hall I have to take pot luck; I cannot be sure how the music sounds. But in the recording studio I begin with the conception of the inner ear. Then I hear the sound of the instrument as affected by the studio, the sound damped and hopelessly padded if the studio is a dry one, or confused and abnormally sonorous if the studio is resonant. After that, the conception of the inner ear has to be checked with what is actually picked up by the microphone and registered on the tape that one hears on the playback. (There is a further dimension over which I alas have no control, namely what each individual playback machine and player does to the record once it is produced.)

The inner ear is the repository of what one has captured in one's best moments, and a fund of insurance to help salvage one's worst. It is, in short, the storehouse of inspiration.

The Technical Approach

Technique bears almost the same relation to the inner ear as deed to word, and is clearly indispensable to the functioning of an interpreter.[1] Obviously complete control of fingers is needed both in matters of timing and of nuance. One needs to be able to press the key at the exact moment intended and to lift it precisely when it is desirable to do so. On instruments capable of inflection one must have complete control over all gradations of nuance. Obviously, total agility and a complete independence of the ten fingers are necessary. Here I am speaking of a frankly modern technique designed for all purposes.

My own views about finger technique are affected by a desire to deal with both the harpsichord and the clavichord and by the necessity to use a great variety of different instruments. I once owned at the same time four harpsichords that demanded totally different re-

1. Kirkpatrick, Ralph: "Fifty Years of Harpsichord Playing," *Early Music*, Vol. 11 [January 1983], pp. 31–41.

sources of touch, registration, and phrasing in order to reproduce in some measure what I heard in my inner ear. It is understandable that careful and consistent fingerings are of great advantage in going from one instrument to another. They are also an enormous help to the memory. The careless and inefficient fingerings of many organists originate in their habit of playing from music and thereby escaping some of the direct consequences of those awkward shifts of hand position and of unnecessary substitution of fingers that can trip up a performer who is playing from memory.

I built up my own keyboard technique very largely on the exercises of Hummel's piano method of 1828, which contains an admirably organized series of exercises designed to take care of nearly everything that the ten fingers need be expected to negotiate.[2] Of course the common basis for both harpsichord and clavichord is primarily finger technique. Considerations of weight playing are non-existent. The hand carries the fingers; it is the job of the fingers to depress and lift the keys. The more independence there is among the fingers, the more one has control over polyphony and over the tiny motions which determine precision on the harpsichord and finesse of nuance on the clavichord.

I use a frankly modern system of fingering, one that avoids unnecessary shifts of hand position and provides the possibility of continuous legato whether or not it is needed. This makes it very much easier to go from a non-sustaining instrument to a sustaining one. The only reason why I can achieve any kind of legato on the organ is that in Bach I have always designed every fingering to provide for this possibility. I never sacrifice the possibility of a legato fingering unless I know that I am dealing with a passage that in any version or on any instrument will always need to be played detaché.

It happens that I have large hands so that I can do monstrous things like trilling in legato octaves in either hand. In Bach this serves me to little purpose, but the stretching comes in handy in some of the more formidable of the fingerbreaking fugues. But when a pupil with small hands says, "But *you* can reach that," my answer is that there is always a fingering which may not provide a universal com-

2. Hummel, J. N.: *Ausführliche theoretisch-practische Anweisung zum Piano-Forte-Spiel*, . . . Wien . . . 1828.

mand of legato but which will nevertheless accomplish its purpose. One must never give up hope for a workable fingering, even if one has hands only half the size of mine.

Once a careful fingering has been made, departures from it are very likely to take place. In returning to pieces which I had fingered while learning them, I sometimes discover that I have simplified the fingering in one way or other. But when I have made changes in an already consistent fingering, the changes themselves are usually consistent. I no longer find myself in that perilous position of changing the fingering each time I play a given passage. If it turns out that one's fingering is changing on every repetition of a piece, there is no help but to write in fingerings, even though they may never again be literally followed. The act of writing down a fingering somehow precipitates a final set of consistent decisions. (To designate a text into which the editor has written fingerings as an Urtext seems to be an act of flagrant dishonesty. Any serious player or anyone who expects to get beyond the level of mere sight-reading should be prepared at all times to supply his own fingerings.)

Along with complete agility and control of the fingers goes the need for the greatest possible economy of motion. One should never do something in two gestures that can be accomplished in one. Too much keyboard playing is riddled with unnecessary movements. My system of finger technique is applicable not only to the harpsichord and the clavichord, but also to the organ, where the motions of the hand could and should be reduced to a minimum.

There exist distressingly great discrepancies between what one feels about music in terms of vehemence of expression and expansiveness of gesture, and the limited and artificial movements which produce that music from a keyboard instrument. When one would like to leap three feet in the air, what can one do? One has only the possibility of making the tiny motion that will produce an upbeat staccato. Something may call for a simple and unbroken musical continuity and yet be executable only by a complicated set of finger and hand adjustments. It is fairly easy to reconstruct the vocal feel of a single line by adapting it to the continuity of an exhalation of breath. It can be made to fit just as closely as if it were being sung. An organ pedal part or its equivalent in a single line on the keyboard can be brought very close to the physical sensation of walking. But in three- and four-voice writing neither the inherent vocal sense of the lines nor the implications of physical movement correspond to the actual gesture of keyboard playing.

One might say that with inner hearing, there is a set of ideal gestures that govern (or should govern) everything that one is doing at the keyboard. Once one gets the feel of a given gesture, it is possible to preserve the feel of executing it even while resorting to gestures that are quite different. The performance will be all the more effective if one can translate the feel of a staccato upbeat leaping three feet into the air into the drastically reduced space of a mere quarter inch, or if one can find the movement that will express the total unbroken continuity of not only one voice or phrase, but of several phrases at once, in a unifying, all-pervasive imaginary gesture. Even when complicated motions are involved, an inner gesture can be found that will control the absolute unity of movements that one undertakes to execute.

Perhaps the easiest gesture of all to perform is the circle, because it is totally continuous, and has a built-in unity. I often ask pupils to describe continuous circles in order to acquire the feeling of an unbroken continuity. In the human organism, any sense of continuity of gesture or movement is derived from the solar plexus, from the diaphragm. One may sit down in a chair and get up from it in one or in several pieces, depending on whether or not the movement has been dominated by the solar plexus. Stage performers and choreographers will know what I mean. Any good actor or any good dancer knows infinitely more about this than I.

None of these gestures can be made without its appropriate preparation in the solar plexus. I cited earlier the example of lifting the hand without preparing that lifting. It is impossible, since the destiny of any gesture depends on the nature of its preparation. This is why it is so much more important to manipulate what happens immediately before arriving at a moment of supreme importance rather than to wait until after that moment has arrived. Any sportsman knows this, and certainly any dancer who wishes to avoid falling flat on his face every time he moves. Babies find this out when they learn to walk.

I have said before that the harpsichord and the clavichord are both finger-technique instruments, but there are enormous differences within this common characteristic. The harpsichord, while basically a non-inflecting instrument like the organ, is susceptible of more nuance than is commonly thought. One can bring the string into vibration quickly or slowly. While this does not permit continuous crescendos and diminuendos, it does permit some differentiation in terms of accent and tapering of harmonic resolutions.

The more stops one draws on a properly regulated harpsichord, the more the touch can be influenced. A properly regulated harpsichord is one in which the various registers speak almost imperceptibly one after the other. (It is a tremendous mistake to adjust a harpsichord so that all registers sound at once when a key is depressed. In that case, there is no control over the touch. Everything has to be hammered out. But it is possible to influence the sonority if the attacks of the different registers are staggered in the following order: four-foot, lower eight-foot, upper eight-foot.) On most harpsichords a quick blow will usually bring out more four-foot than eight-foot tone. A slower attack can be used to set the eight-foot strings in vibration a little more slowly, and since they have a tendency to determine the character of the tutti, the sound then becomes fuller and more mellow. Although these differences are very slight, they cannot be disregarded.[3]

By and large the determining factor on the harpsichord is not so much touch as timing, the starting and stopping of notes with a precision of which many instrumentalists never dream. There is, however, a variation in the resistance of harpsichord keys between bass and treble, which depends on whether or not keyboards have been coupled or on the number of sets of plectra plucking strings. The overall standardization that pianists have been led to expect from a well-regulated Steinway is absent. Instead of relying on the instrument, one must have control of the fingers at all times.[4]

It is unwise to use weight, or to throw the finger in such fashion that one temporarily loses control of it, as happens with so many

---

3. These remarks and the possibilities they outline are contradicted by a formerly and once again current, and unfortunately widespread, fashion of staggering the attacks of the various registers so that the four-foot sounds last.
4. Another fashion now unfortunately current is that of reducing to a minimum the resistance of the harpsichord key in all registers, with the result that most of the possibilities of touch and articulation are irretrievably lost.

techniques of piano playing. Nor can one rely on the weight of the key to bring the finger back up. One has to manipulate the touch so as to send the plectrum past the string at the precise time desired. Otherwise, if there is unevenness in the instrument, there will be unevenness in the playing. The watchword in harpsichord playing is control of the fingers at all times, control such that once the plectrum has been sent past the string, only enough pressure is kept on the key to ensure its remaining depressed for the desired length of time. Under no circumstances should one "keybed." Any excess of pressure should cease immediately after the plucking of the string. Nothing sounds worse on the harpsichord, incidentally, than a kind of loose, bouncy staccato, carried over from the piano. It has no body at all. If a staccato that really has a shape is desired, it must be controlled.

On the clavichord, touch is everything, touch and control over nuance.[5] It is the only keyboard instrument on which the tone can be controlled after the key has been depressed. The tangent, at the end of a simple key lever, is in direct contact with the string. Thus it is possible to raise the pitch, or by rapid alternation of pressure and release to produce a kind of vibrato or *Bebung*, one which corresponds, however, to only half of the string player's vibrato, since the pitch can only be raised, never lowered.

Without a clavichord technique it is almost as hard to judge a clavichord as a violin under comparable circumstances. One can scratch on the most beautiful Stradivarius, and one can produce unpleasant sounds on the best clavichord. As on stringed instruments, one really does manufacture one's own tone color.

On the clavichord, the extent of key dip is almost never more than an eighth of an inch. If the note is not approached from the surface of the key, one has no control whatsoever over the tone. This means that the whole operating area represents only a fraction of that afforded by the average harpsichord, and much less than that which is available on the piano. In brilliant detaché passages on the average harpsichord it is sometimes expedient to lift one's fingers very high. This does not work on the clavichord. One has to maintain contact with the key at all times, and to employ a kind of totally rubbery

5. Kirkpatrick, Ralph: "On Playing the Clavichord," *Early Music*, Vol. 9 [July 1981], pp. 293–305.

touch. One of the most important precautions in beginning to play the clavichord is never to allow a bad sound to be produced. The instrument is so sensitive that if a set of bad habits is built up, the chances of getting rid of them are very slim. It goes almost without saying that any continued excess of pressure on a clavichord key can cause the tone to go sharp as the tangent on the string increases its tension to more than normal. Clearly, here "keybedding" in the manner of all too many pianists finds its logical conclusion in broken strings!

About the organ or the piano, I cannot speak with comparable authority but I do think that a good harpsichord technique would do many organists a great deal of good. It seems to me that one needs just as much independence of fingers on the organ as on the harpsichord in order to command the phrasing of polyphony. I have great doubts, however, about the possibility of really good polyphonic playing on the modern piano unless one also has well-developed fingers. Even though one can play very beautifully while wearing mittens (there are techniques that function in comparable fashion, particularly those involving rotation and failure to articulate the finger joints), it is useless to pretend that the mitten allows the hand its maximum freedom, especially in dealing with polyphony. But sometimes the power of an inner conception and a determination to express it can overcome self-created obstacles and even those caused by poor tools. It is entertaining to speculate that the development of keyboard playing from the early organ to the modern carillon, progressing from alternating unarticulated hands by way of a walking two-by-two fingering to the complete articulation and functioning of all ten fingers, has now come full circle; a history of keyboard techniques might well be entitled *From Fist to Fist*.

The Formation of an Interpretation

As a sample, convenient for its relative brevity, I propose to reconstruct the formation of an interpretation of the A minor Prelude of Book I. Here I shall attempt to recall everything with which I have ever had to deal in preparing its performance. This sample may also serve as a review of much to which allusion has been made in preceding pages. Of course, the sequence narrated here is imposed for the sake of clarity. All of this might arrive instinctively, at the very first sight-reading.

A first encounter with the piece takes the form of a preliminary sight-reading, a non-committal acquaintance with the notes. Withholding any definite decisions, and attempting to avoid the formation of any habits, I try to get the general feel of the piece. Then it is time to find out what to do with the fingering. If it does not reveal itself automatically and consistently, I write in the necessary indications. If later I discover that I have written in a bad fingering, I improve on it. By this time I have mastered the notes so that I can play the piece in time and at a plausible tempo, even the one which I may finally choose.

Then perhaps I begin to think about the rhythmic shape of the piece and to explore its rhythmic syllabization. Working voice by voice and starting, as nearly always, with the bass, I will mark the beginnings of the rhythmic syllables in the score (Example 6.1). Many of them are self-evident, but a few require some comment. In measure 4 and 8 the decorated afterbeat, if regarded as fundamentally a continuation of the previous eighth-note motion, hardly constitutes a new syllable. In measure 5 I have inserted a tie which is not present in Kroll's Bachgesellschaft text. At the beginning of measure 13 two syllables overlap on the first E, which represents the end of one and the beginning of the other. In such cases, an articulation is usually desirable. A parallel passage occurs in measure 22. In measure 26, if the last group of sixteenth notes is regarded as representing a continuation of eighth-note motion into the first beat of measure 27, the new syllable would start on the second sixteenth of measure 27, as it does in the tenor in that same measure. One further rhythmic element that heightens the expressiveness of measures 16–20, already harmonically and tonally the most eloquent of the entire piece, is Bach's use of slower motion in the soprano.

In considering melodic intervals I have the alternatives of regarding this Prelude as a predominantly two-voice piece, or as a melodically decorated wash of harmony. In the latter case many notes might well be prolonged beyond their written value, thereby reducing the melodic content to a minimum and stressing predominantly the harmonic underpinning. If, however, I decide that the piece is predominantly melodic, I then sing everything in all voices, so that the vocal feel of each interval can be ascertained.

Example 6.1 Prelude A minor, I

Example 6.1 (*Continued*)

At this point, if not sooner, it will be time to consider the harmonic substructure and to identify the simplest possible harmonies to which this piece can be reduced. (See Example 6.2.) Measures 1–8 contain one chord per measure. Then the harmonic motion begins to accelerate in measures 9–11, with two chords per measure. It then slows up in measures 12–16 with one chord per measure. The fundamental harmony assumes a slightly different rhythm in measures 17 and 19, because the change of chord occurs on the second instead of the third part of the measure as in measures 9–11. Measures 20–23 have only one chord per measure, but in measure 24 the movement of the bass, D–B–G-sharp, creates an acceleration of harmonic movement, and in the last three measures, we return to one harmony per measure.

We might look now for what can be extracted in terms of consonance and dissonance. Our first harmonic phrase consists of a consonance, dissonance, and consonance (measures 1–4), and the second phrase is built on the same pattern. From measure 9 the pattern changes and there are no predominant basic dissonances until mea-

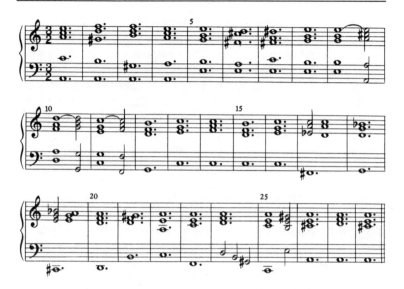

Example 6.2 Prelude A minor, I, harmonic reduction

sure 17. Here it becomes rather intense. From measure 21 on, all
dissonances are used to reestablish the A minor tonic and the subdominant and dominant of its cadence. In other words, the dissonant
content of this piece has its own specific shape.

We might then look at the shape of the tonal plan. The first phrase
is obviously in A minor (measure 4), followed by the minor dominant for the second phrase (measures 5–8). But in measures 9–10
we begin to modulate into a clear C major, which we keep until we
trouble it with an excursion into G minor by way of a diminished
seventh on F-sharp (measure 17). This is the first onset of a pathos
that continues into the D minor subdominant (measures 19–20).
Thereafter we have merely to draw the piece to a conclusion, with
some reminiscent dissonances. That is our broad outline.

Let us see what happens with the small dissonances, cross relations, and diagonal relationships. We begin with a passing note, and
a set of changing notes which already lend a certain intensification
to the first measure. If we wished to express the tapered-off afterbeat
in measure 4, we might make use of some of the passing notes it

contains. Our first modulatory tone, however, is the D-sharp in measure 4. And there are also expressive intervals which could be brought
out. The second phrase has the same pattern as the first. On looking
at it, however, we note the dissonances: in measure 5, A against G
and against E (which is the real bass), F-sharp against the still-
dominating influence of the real bass, E. There is a passing note
again in measure 6, now in the bass, and a changing note in measure
7, soprano. Here we become really quite pathetic, particularly if we
hear the E, not against the C, but against the F-sharp in the bass. If
we decide that they are necessary to the fundamental expression of
the piece, quite a few clashes can be extracted from this measure. In
measures 9–12 there are a number of passing notes which can be
heard in various ways. However, if we wish to express the relaxation
into C major (measure 13) we must not weigh the passage down by
exaggerating its dissonant elements. They can be allowed merely to
shimmer instead.

From measure 17, however, if the passing notes are underlined
against the main harmony and all the performer's inhibitions are cast
off, an intensity can be achieved reminiscent of the Chopin A-flat
major Prelude. (See Example 6.3.) It is very easy to say that a good

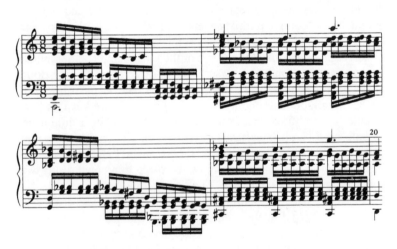

Example 6.3 Prelude A minor, I, rewritten

interpretation is only based on what is really in the music, but so, in one sense, was the foregoing.

Yet the dissonances can become even richer as we arrive at the passage following measure 24, especially if chords are filled up and octaves doubled in both hands, in the style of Rachmaninoff at his most self-indulgent. (See Example 6.4.) If one heard this piece on the piano without any indication that it was by Bach, it might make a very satisfactory example of musical vehemence. What should keep me from perpetrating this? For one thing, the experience I have of the harpsichord and clavichord shows me immediately that this conception cannot possibly work on either instrument. Therefore it can not have been in Bach's mind either.

But all exaggerations aside, the question arises as to the characterization that is to be given to this prelude. Is it merely a two-voice piece for oboe and bassoon? Is it a solo? Certainly, on the surface, this looks like a piece for solo sound. This is the impression it gives me on the clavichord. Nor would I like to hear it registered otherwise on the harpsichord. In any case, its relationship to the subsequent fugue requires some consideration especially since the massive tex-

Example 6.4 Prelude A minor, I, rewritten

ture of the fugue can hardly be regarded as demanding anything but something other than a mere solistic sound.

The Later Life of an Interpretation, or Inspiration and Its Vicissitudes

Here we have to consider what may happen to an initial interpretation in the course of arriving at a routined performance that can be produced under any circumstances, and how its initial inspiration can ultimately be recaptured. Usually, in the course of routining, the inspiration becomes a little battle-worn. After the conception of an interpretation, even if one has a great deal of facility and a perfectly adequate technique, one can usually expect some very bad days. The routining of unconscious control of physical motions and the preparing to be able to play the piece under any adverse circumstances, can dull the freshness of a performance. Even that sacred repository of inspiration, the inner ear, may be invaded by the automatisms of routine practicing. It may become much more necessary to cultivate one's hearing than one's fingers.

If one is playing the *WTC* one is faced with the problem of playing a set of pieces that were never intended for public performance. Bach himself gives little help because he is so consistently untheatrical. There is a kind of expectation, even on the part of the most sophisticated audiences, that anyone who walks out on a stage alone will produce some sort of a show, and if he doesn't, there usually results an atmosphere of dullness and disappointment. Nobody expects a string quartet to act that way, but the curse of the expected shenanigan hangs over every solo appearance.

Something else which is potentially quite disconcerting, assuming that all else comes off well, is the effect that these pieces can have in relation to their sequence. So much depends on what comes before and what comes after, and on the general tone of the program. The problem of producing any one of these pieces so that it can be really heard for itself parallels the problem that a gallery director has in exhibiting paintings so that each can be seen by itself. If one makes too pretty a show, too successful a program, very often the individual piece gets lost, just as the perfectly hung painting can be absorbed by the decorative scheme to which it contributes. Often it happens that a piece functions in a program only because of the sound it happens to be making at that particular time. Furthermore, in public performance of the *WTC*, one is faced with the fact that there is no one instrument adequate for the purpose. They all furnish only miserable approximations of the musical content, and the performer is walking a kind of tightrope between the ideal and the practical. The means of communicating the ideal through the practical are perilous indeed. Again, the imagination and the inner ear must at all times stand ready for the rescue.

It is easy to mistake self-indulgence for inspiration. All religious disciplines know that it is sometimes exceedingly difficult to distinguish between the voice of God and the voice of the Devil. No matter how much we listen to our inner voices, we need to listen to other people's voices too in order to make sure that we have been genuinely inspired, not merely self-indulgent.

Ideals of Interpretation

In order to formulate a few ideals of interpretation, it might be well to assume that to find out what something really is and why one likes it, there is no better way than to examine what it clearly is not and to assess one's unfavorable reactions. History has furnished us with many examples of faith reinforced by the persecution of unbelievers. I shall proceed here to eliminate from further consideration a few kinds of performance.

No time need be wasted on the primitive stages of technical incompetence or inadequate musical comprehension even though they are considered to have a certain charm when exhibited on old instruments. Such performances have the further advantage that when the performer understands very little, he is unlikely to trouble the audience with anything that it too cannot understand. We can also dispense with what I call the parrot performances, namely those which are highly routined and dictated at first hand by a coach or at second hand by an editor, but which in no way represent any deep or independent musical thinking. Some of these, especially on the piano, are what one might call "traditional" performances. In such performances the player emits a series of pretty sounds and refrains from playing too loudly because it might be considered unBachish, nor does he double any octaves because it might be considered "not in style."

Somewhat more difficult to eliminate are the performances of Bach used as a vehicle for the exhibition of borrowed trappings. The performer plays colored lights on the sacred name of Bach and pockets the applause and the box-office receipts. The only people who have any right to use Bach as a "vehicle" are those who are above doing so, artists of the quality of a Busoni or a Webern. These "vehicle" performances are virtually indistinguishable from the sensational performances that are designed at every possible moment and by every possible means to stun the audience. It may well be answered that a sensational performance is exactly what one wants. But there are different levels and different kinds of sensationalism, and some are obviously closer than others to Bach's intentions.

In reaction to the sensational performance we are often offered the "authentic" performance. This type is hard to dispose of, because it has a tendency to include the audience in an exercise of moral virtue that leads it to mistake boredom for edification. It reminds me of a glass case containing a tasteful display of archeological remains; but the word *tasteful* is perhaps misplaced, for I do not think taste even enters into the "authentic" performance. Too often historical authenticity can be used as a means of escape from any potentially disquieting observance of esthetic values, and from the assumption of any genuine artistic responsibility. The abdication of esthetic values and artistic responsibilities can confer a certain illusion of simplicity on what the passage of history has presented to us, bleached as white as bones on the sands of time. We are all familiar with those simplistic notions with which it has become customary to regard the ancient Greeks. Some of us are capable of imagining a welcome objectivity in sixteenth-century music sung without any expression or any artistry whatsoever. A certain attractiveness is to be found in the notion that it has been rendered unproblematical. Whether or not Bach is a composer to render unproblematical is anyone's privilege to decide.

To conclude the list of candidates for the trash heap, we have the so-called definitive performance. Even though one can say that a performance of breathtaking beauty is already a miracle, one can say that a definitive performance is an impossibility. Only stillborn music can receive definitive performances. (This after all could and frequently should be considered tantamount to burial.) Yet one often hears talk of "definitive" performances from those who pontificate confidently and grandly, as do record reviewers and those excessively addicted to the use of the phonograph, in pitting one "definitive" performance against another while comparing mere details, without the necessary comprehension of the essential elements and forces which work to shape these performances.

Interpretation functions between two extremes. One extreme is indicated by the text and by the composer's supposed intentions, in other words, by the work itself. The other extreme is indicated by the contribution, often necessary and desirable, of the interpreter and by the liberties that he is entitled to take. One of the extremes can be regarded as fixed and obligatory, as a firmly established point of departure; the other extreme can be regarded as created by the infinitely variable possibilities of interpretation and by the play of choice and fantasy around the structure that the composer has given us. The composer has indicated an ideal constellation of forces, which bring about results which even he himself cannot always predict. Thus like a living organism every valid work of art reveals potentialities that are as unforeseen by its creator as are the careers of children by their parents.

Variable balancing of musical elements permits a wide divergence among interpretive choices and among the resulting performances. What is found to be most important in a given piece is dependent on what most appeals to the performer's own personality. Many of these interpretive choices are perfectly legitimate and will legitimately continue to occur. One might say that the composer is the choreographer, the interpreter the dancer. The necessarily personal experience of a work which a performer has to communicate imports a certain amount of commentary on his part, whether overt or tacit. It can happen that the performer's contribution carries itself beyond exaggeration into distortion. Yet the commentaries and distortions of some interpreters are more interesting than those of others. There are exaggerations and distortions that grow out of a serious grappling with artistic problems, out of a genuinely creative musical thinking, in contrast to the superficial traits, the petty stamps of ownership, the mannerisms that are often mistaken for style.

It is the miraculous power of a work like the *WTC*, and many others, to survive its own time and context, to adapt to changing interpretations, and to surmount misunderstanding and deformation. It has those qualities which give it the possibility of perpetual renewal and which prevent it from ever being rendered completely meaningless. In short, as has so often been said, it is immortal. Colloquially stated: You can't kill it!

My own ideal of interpretation is one of respectful freedom, one that encourages the organic flowering of a work out of itself in the course of a free and vital interaction of its own elements. It presupposes a certain distinction between what is obligatory and unquestionable, and what is up to the choice and whim of the performer. Yet once the fundamental premises of the work are understood and respected, there is nothing that can be too eloquently stated. The only limitations are those imposed by the nature of the instrument and by the proportions and character of the piece. Overstatement of details can sometimes produce understatement of a work as a whole. Yet how often can significant understatement add up to overwhelming eloquence!

My conception of expression varies from that of my first piano teachers. Their admonition was, Learn the notes and then put in the expression. (Shades of the harmonium swell and of the player piano of 1919!) My admonition is to learn the notes and understand their relationships, and then to draw the expression out. I reiterate my earlier statement that no musical expression exists that addresses itself only to the ear. It addresses itself to the entire body and its meaning concerns our entire being.

One may ask: toward whom is a performance directed? For what audience does one shape one's interpretations? I can only answer: for my peers, for those whose taste and sensibilities are on a level commensurate with my own artistic endeavor; and for my betters, those whose capacities of perception approach those of the composer. One has the obligation to communicate as clearly and as compellingly as possible, but never knowingly to talk down or to force the music to descend below its own level. If there are inherent elements that will stun the gentlefolk, by all means make full use of them! But do not introduce them where they do not belong. And above all, talk no unnecessary baby talk. I would not wish to deprive those listeners whose capacities are worthy of this music of any of its possible meaning. Let others seize what they can. If integrity is present, even if they do not understand it, they will nevertheless somehow sense it. To be really serious, without resorting to solemnity, let us paraphrase an old saying: Nothing is good enough, when all our efforts and all our desires are directed toward a communication of what mirrors the best that is conceivable to man. This certainly holds good for the *WTC*, which, much as it both invites and defies interpretation, remains infinitely revealing, infinitely inscrutable, and totally irreplaceable.

Index

Accent, 69
Agogics. *See* Articulation; Phrasing
Articulation, 61–63, 84, 87

Basso continuo. *See* Thoroughbass
Busoni, Ferruccio, 19, 47

Cadence, 95–96, 102–03
Chromatic Fantasy, 90, 102
Clavichord: performing *WTC* upon, 44; technique of, 116–17
Clavier, problems of meaning, 8–9
Cross-relations, 98–99, 100; examples of, 121–22

Diagonal relationship. *See* Cross-relations
Dissonance, Bach's use of, 93, 96, 101. *See also* Cross-relations; Suspension
Double dotting, 27
Downbeat, preparation for, 68
Dynamics, 62, 106–07

Figured bass. *See* Thoroughbass
Fingerings, 22, 59–60, 111–13
Fischer, Johann Caspar Ferdinand, 7
Fugal subjects: contours of, 52–53; contrapuntal structure of, 55–56; melodic elaboration of, 56–57, 78

Gerber, Ernst Ludwig, 5

Harpsichord: "Bach instrument," 10; registration, 10, 42–44, 103, 115; technique of, 111–17

Mattheson, Johann, 7
Melodic syllables, 63

Ornamentation, 23–26

Piano, as instrument for performing *WTC*, 44–45
Pasquali, Nicolo, 39–41
Phrasing, 61–63, 86–87

Reger, Max, 20
Rhythm: distinguished from meter, 69; problems of, 70–75
Rhythmic syllables: definition of, 76; variety of length, 78; example of, 118–19
Ritard, 82
Rubato, 68

Suspension, 99–100
Syncopation, 78

Tempo, 26–27, 46–47, 67, 85–86
Thoroughbass: significance to Bach's harmony, 90, 92, 100, 104–05; classification of chords, 92–93

131